Invitations

to the

Dance

Invitations
to the
Dance

sermons that celebrate life

by Michael W. Brown

Universalist Unitarian Church
of Peoria, Illinois

Published by the Universalist Unitarian Church of Peoria, Illinois
Printed in the United States of America

"**The Secret**" by Denise Levertov, from POEMS 1960-1967, copyright © 1964 by Denise Levertov, is reprinted by permission of New Directions Publishing Corp. U.S./Canadian rights only

Quotation from *Encountering God* by Diana L. Eck is copyrighted © 1993, 2003, by Diana L. Eck and is reprinted by permission of Beacon Press, Boston.

The author, editor, and publisher would like to express their gratitude to David Brown for his fine renderings of the ancient drawings used in "Better Living Through Alchemy."

Edited by Jean Slonneger
Copyedited by Kathy Carter
Book design by Jean Slonneger

ISBN 0-9762246-1-5

This book is dedicated to my family: Daniel, David, Diane, Jean, and Paul

Acknowledgements

My thanks go out to the wonderful members and friends of the Universalist Unitarian Church of Peoria for their many acts of kindness to me, and particularly for listening to my sermons over the years. It's a great thing to be listened to; we could all use more of that experience. In addition, for the comments, the feedback, the dialogue, and the companionship, I say a heartfelt thanks. Jean Slonneger, my editor, was absolutely crucial to the completion of this book. She did a marvelous job, and it quite literally would not have happened without her. Many thanks also to Kathy Carter for her helpful suggestions for wording. And David Brown did a great job as illustrator. I am indeed fortunate to be surrounded by so many helpful friends.

—Michael

Contents

Foreword

by Rev. David Robins

Opening and reading this book of sermons should be like sitting down and listening to a good story. These sermons contain stories that will let you get to know a good minister in the very heartland of the country. Michael "plays in Peoria," and his success as a minister in this lovely city along the Illinois River is a testament to his deep-felt calling of the spirit.

Like the river, Michael carries the heavy loads of ministering to people, challenging conventions, and speaking for love and justice from his pulpit. He also carries the heavy load of being a lifelong Chicago Cubs fan, long-suffering, but with a graceful sense of humor about those lovable losers. I admire him for placing his sermons into the larger world. He is not afraid to "swing for the wall"!

I have known Michael for almost twenty years. He is dedicated to his family, to the ministry, and to playing the banjo. He may not admit it, but he belongs to a pickup bluegrass band composed of other ministers, named Negotiated Settlement. Fortunately, all of the band members have been blessed with not having to be part of a negotiated settlement from their churches! It was just like him to be the instrumental player in getting the ministers together to play music. He lives his life in this way, and his spirit comes through in his sermons. He brings people together for a higher purpose, without forcing them or manipulating them.

He is a true uniter, and you will learn more about the nature of uniting people and ideas in these sermons.

Michael writes in the tradition of Unitarian Universalism, speaking to the principles of worth and dignity and to the virtues of Truth and Beauty. He writes from the passions of his heart passed through the firing clarity of his thinking.

Michael speaks personally of his own wrestling with the challenges of the day. He also speaks in language and ideas that are universally meaningful and true. When you read this collection of sermons, I encourage you to picture yourself in Michael's UU Church sanctuary, he in the pulpit, welcoming you with his smile.

David Robins, D.Min, is minister of the Unitarian Universalist Church of Bloomington-Normal, Illinois.

Jane Ising, a member of our church, celebrated her 100th birthday on February 2, 2002. Among her many birthday parties was one we held for her at church. I could not resist using her amazing life in this sermon as a model of what might be possible for all of us. —MB

How to Fashion a Life

April 14, 2002

What a great day it is to be able to celebrate Jane Ising's 100th birthday with her. I appreciate Jane's willingness to let us share a little bit of her birthday experience with us. She wouldn't want me to talk about her too much, but her life is an inspiring story for us and quite naturally encourages all of us to think about our own lives and to consider carefully what matters most to us.

There is a wonderful story by J. D. Salinger called *Teddy*, which I highly recommend to you. I won't tell you the whole story, but it should suffice to say that Teddy is a very precocious 10-year-old, and throughout the story Salinger gives us some of the priceless insights of this young fellow. During the story Teddy has a lengthy philosophical discussion with a psychologist about what is really important in life. At one point in the discussion, Teddy asks the psychologist if he is familiar with the expression "gift horse," as in the proverb "never look a gift horse in the mouth." When the psychologist says that he is, Teddy responds by saying, "Life is a gift horse in my opinion."

Life is, in fact, a gift, whether we can actually pinpoint the giver or not. Life is given to us. It just shows up and here we are—living, breathing, conscious beings—faced with a kaleidoscope of sights and sounds, an often confusing inheritance of traditions and customs, some pretty nontrivial challenges, a body that can do all sorts of amazing things, and a sometimes overwhelming array of options, decisions, and choices to be made at almost every moment, day in and day out, until we die.

It's a paradoxical gift, no doubt, full of both joy and sorrow, pleasure and pain, and yet also full of a magnificence that inspires our awe and sometimes even our worship. Life is a gift horse, indeed. A gift horse that eats all your food, kicks over the fence, breaks your heart when it dies, and yet is incredibly beautiful and vibrant and inspiring. Such is life. Overall, very few of the recipients would rather not have this paradoxical gift.

When we know someone like Jane who has lived what seems to us to be a truly worthwhile life, I think it's inspiring to us. It makes us realize what an amazing thing a human life is, how complex, how subtle, how rich, how multifaceted, and at times how downright difficult. And we are genuinely inspired by someone like Jane who seems to have navigated all kinds of difficult waters and

14

has come through so well, with such grace and so fruitfully. Jane, you really do us a service simply by being our friend and by being such a great example to us all.

It was Socrates who declared that the unexamined life is not worth living. We are beings with consciousness. We have the qualities of self-awareness and self-reflection. These qualities are part of the unique gift of human life. Life seems to invite us to ponder it. It almost seems to require that we do so. Not to just go here or there at random, but to think, to feel, to reason, to choose, to discern what is the best path at any given moment of decision.

One could pass one's time in so many ways—as a criminal, as an artist, as a scientist, as a person of commerce, as a complainer, as a saint. Part of the gift of life is that we are invited to make choices; we are invited to fashion our lives, within certain boundaries, in the way that seems best to us. This seems to me to be the crux of the matter, this array of possibilities and our freedom to choose what to

"Life seems to invite us to ponder it. It almost seems to require that we do so. Not to just go here or there at random, but to think, to feel, to reason, to choose, to discern what is the best path at any given moment of decision."

us seems best—and of course, along with that freedom, the responsibility to accept the consequences of our choices. What is it that matters most? What is it that matters least? These are the questions we are called to answer in examining our lives and making our choices.

I'd like to offer a few personal reflections on how these priorities play out for me. I don't present them as dogma or as universal truths, but as working principles that make sense to me at this time in my life. I can't be sure they will work perfectly for you, but that's part of the gift: we each have to figure out our answers to these questions for ourselves. And yet there are common themes in our lives that seem to be surprisingly universal for us all.

If any one quest seems to be central in human life, including my own, it's the quest for love. As James Taylor says, "There's no doubt in anybody's mind that love's the finest thing around."

And so for most of us, the search for love in its many forms is central to our lives. We live out this search in our choosing of partners, in our relationships with children and parents and grandparents and siblings, and with our friends.

When the search for love goes well in our lives, it's like finding cool water in the desert. Love is amazingly satisfying, and the lack of it is an enormous deprivation. As we search for and sometimes find love, we almost without exception get hurt somewhere along the way, and our ability to withstand these hurts and rebound back from them is crucial if we're to find satisfaction in life. Our ability to give and receive love—with partners, with parents and children, with siblings, and with friends—is an essential factor in the quality of our living. There's just nothing like love.

Freud claimed that the two big issues of life are love and work. Although I will argue for more than two, he certainly seems to be right in putting work near the top. Each of us must find some satisfying work to do in this world—"right livelihood," the Buddhists call it. Hopefully our work does more than just earn us a living, although earning a living is important. People who love their work are fortunate indeed, and those who hate their work are far too numerous.

"Our ability to give and receive love . . . is an essential factor in the quality of our living."

Finding one's work is not a simple or obvious thing. I didn't make the final decision to go into the ministry until I was 40. That's a long time to be thinking things over. But still, I'm one of the lucky ones because I found something that I like to do. It makes life a lot more enjoyable.

That's the end of Freud's list, but I would add a few more items. One is what we might call "right action," or we might call it being an ethical person. I don't think it's possible to live a deeply satisfying life if we're not concerned about ethics, goodness, and justice. To live a good life is to be concerned about whether others are having a good life too. It's to be concerned with one's neighbor, one's community, with universal issues, not just what Ezra Pound called "one's own personal bellyaches." So for me this element of concerned, ethical living goes on the list as an essential element of a truly good life.

> *"To live a good life is to be concerned about whether others are having a good life too."*

I would also add the element of play to my list of what makes a good life. I think we need to be able to let go of seriousness sometimes, to relax, to lay our burdens down, to just have fun in many ways: concerts, theater, travel, sports, and so on. I feel I've been moderately successful with this dimension of life, and one of the things I like about this church is that we seem to know how to play. Some folks never develop this skill, and they don't tend to be the happiest folks in the world. All work and no play makes Jill a dull girl.

I have just one more item to put on my personal list, and I'm not sure what to call it. We might call it "spirituality," but I'm not sure that's exactly the right word. I think it has to do with our relationship to life itself—our response to the gift of life taken as a whole.

Forrest Church, a UU minister and well-known author, says that "religion is our response to the reality of being alive and the knowledge that we have to die." What is our response to the gift of life with all its ambiguity and fragility? What is our response to the cosmos itself, to the unimaginably huge and complex creative process of which we are tiny, tiny little parts? Are we mad about it, or are we madly in love with it? Do we see it as primarily awe-inspiring or pointless? Does it fill us with a sense of meaning or one of despair?

How do we respond to the whole package that is our precious, ambiguous gift? We might call this our spiritual life, or we might call it something else; but by whatever name, it is an aspect of being alive that calls out for our response. What is that response, and how do we go about expressing that response in our lives? That for me is an important question, and it seems to be fairly important for many others as well. As a matter of fact, I would suggest that this is what religion is all about—our response to the gift of life.

So that would be my list for how to fashion a truly good and satisfying life. Love, work, right action or "goodness," play, and—for lack of a better word—spirituality. Each of us, as Socrates said, is called to examine his or her own life and to fashion it, insofar as we are able, into the best life possible. This is life's invitation. This is our responsibility and our opportunity. This is what we are being called to do—called by the very nature of life itself to explore the fullness of the gift we have been given.

The ability to do this well is called wisdom, and such wisdom is precious beyond all reckoning. Fortunately, we are not alone in this rather daunting project. We have friends, we have companions, we have guides, we have examples.

Our friend Jane Ising is one such example, and we are grateful to celebrate life with her today as we all seek together to find and enjoy what is truly best in life. ☙

My years serving on the Planned Parenthood Clergy Advisory Board have challenged me to think about what makes for a healthy ethic of sexuality. At one point I helped develop, with the Planned Parenthood group, a sexual ethics statement that reflects many of these basic values.
—MB

Toward a Healthy Ethic of Sexuality

January 23, 1994

My mother-in-law, who is someone I both like and respect, once told me that I should never begin a sermon by talking about how difficult it is to give sermons or by making any other excuses. "Just jump right in," she said. And, in general, I have taken her advice.

But this week in particular, as Sunday came closer and closer, I really began to ask myself: Why am I doing this? What makes me think that I have something meaningful to say about sexual ethics? On the other hand, there seems to be such mass confusion in our culture about sexuality in general, and about sexual ethics in particular, that there is an urgent need for all of us to engage in some real dialogue on this difficult subject.

We are bombarded each day with huge numbers of sexual images through advertising, popular music, and TV. At the same time, our news media are full of stories about date rape, sexual abuse, sexual harassment, teenage pregnancy, and a host of other sex-oriented problems. One begins to wonder if anyone at all has any wisdom to offer on this subject.

Traditionally, religious institutions have played the role of voicing the values of their cultures on moral issues, including sexuality. And, indeed, many religious institutions are playing that role right now. The religious right is busy fighting sex education in the public schools, and the Catholic Church recently issued a papal encyclical on sexuality.

While I respect these institutions and applaud their willingness to take a moral position on sexuality, I also vigorously disagree with many of their specific positions. The papal encyclical, for example, declares the activities of birth control, masturbation, and homosexuality to be "intrinsically evil." As a religious liberal, not only do I not find birth control, masturbation, and homosexuality to be intrinsically evil, I do not find these activities to be intrinsically immoral or unethical at all. In the case of birth control especially, I find this activity to be not only not intrinsically evil but in many situations a moral imperative.

There is plenty of room in this arena for healthy and respectful disagreement among different religious approaches. We religious liberals are often accused of having a soft or even nonexistent approach to sexual morality, but I don't believe that's accurate. I do believe that we as religious liberals can, and indeed must, come forward with

22

what we believe to be a saner, healthier approach to sexual ethics.

To begin that process, I would like to describe, in very broad brush strokes, what I think this healthy sexual ethic would look like. Of course, I don't speak with any particular ecclesiastical authority. I don't speak for the Unitarian Universalist Association or even for this church. I speak as a human being, as a spouse, as a parent, as a person concerned about my own well-being, my family's well-being, and the well-being of the society I live in. You do not have to follow what I say or even agree with me. But I do hope that together we can work toward an appreciation and understanding of human sexuality that will be fulfilling, healthy, and life-enhancing.

"I tend to judge the ethical value of human actions by the effects they produce. I believe that we should act in such a way as to produce the most beneficial result."

In ethical reflection in general, I tend to think from the perspective of process theology, which makes me what is called a "consequentialist." That means I tend to judge the ethical value of human actions by the effects they produce. I believe that we should act in such a way as to produce the most beneficial result.

But how do we define a "beneficial result"? John Cobb, a theologian I particularly like, called it the "richness of experience." Whitehead called it "enjoyment," which is also a good word, but it should not be confused with simply hedonistic pleasure. What we ought to be trying to maximize at every moment is the enjoyment, the fulfillment, the richness of experience, the deep satisfaction and joy of all creatures, ourselves and others. That is what I take to be the goal. And so I will tend to build an ethical system that looks at various human actions and asks the question: Does this action enhance the richness of experience of all the people affected by it, or does it tend in the other direction, toward pain and suffering? To me, that is the crucial question.

The other assumption I have, which I think is probably implicit in the first one but is worth making explicit, is the good old Unitarian Universalist principle of the worth and dignity of every person. Every person has value and is worthy of respect, and no person can legitimately be used simply as the instrument of another person's desires. Human beings are ends in themselves and not just means to an end.

With this basis, I would like to consider how we might build a healthy ethic of sexuality, one that would seek to respect the worth and dignity of each person while maximizing the well-being and fulfillment of all, to the extent that it is possible to do so.

What would such a sexual ethic look like? Its foundation would be, I think, an affirmation that sexuality is good, that sexuality is a valuable aspect of life, that it is a source of joy and satisfaction, and, indeed, that it is impossible even to imagine the kind of world we live in without sex. Certainly none of us would exist if this were such a world, nor would any of the animals or plants around us. So if this life is good, if it is good to be alive, then sexuality is also good. You can't have one without the other. Therefore, it seems to me that we must reject any system of thought or ethics that regards sexuality itself as intrinsically evil—and certainly we have some of that theology in our Western Christian culture.

This classification of sex as evil has caused a host of problems in our culture. Its effects have distorted our view of not just sexuality but women and the entire natural world as well. Because if sex is bad, then life itself is in some sense also bad. Not a very good place to start, in my opinion. So I affirm sexuality as good, as a natural part of life.

But we must be careful not to take the leap from saying that sexuality is good to saying that every expression of sexuality in every situation is good. I doubt very much whether any of us would subscribe to that theory. Fire is good too. I am very glad that we have fire and especially glad that we have a fire going in the furnace at this very moment. But that does not mean that we can ethically justify going around setting fires all over the place whenever we feel like it. I knew one young man in particular who thought that was his mission in life. He needed to be corrected on that issue. Sexuality—like fire, electricity, and nuclear power—is a powerful force that can either enhance human life or have a destructive effect on it. It is our job as wise people to draw out its life-enhancing power and minimize its destructive effects.

Specifically, in every sexual act, in addition to the opportunity for physical pleasure or pain, we can identify three other kinds of effects. One we may call the emotional effect, both for the participants and for the other people in their lives who may be affected, which could possibly be a considerable number of people. Second is the possibility of beginning a new human life, which is an act with extraordinary consequences for many different people. And third is the possibility of the transmission of disease, a particularly significant effect in this age of AIDS.

"Sexuality . . . is a powerful force that can either enhance human life or have a destructive effect on it."

Every sexual act has effects on a physical level of immediate sensation, and perhaps longer term sensation as well; has emotional effects for the participants, and perhaps for others as well; and carries with it the possibility of procreation, as well as the possibility of transmission of disease. So sexuality is a pretty powerful thing, something to be handled wisely.

I will offer to you five rules with which I think we can begin a discussion with the goal of establishing a healthy sexual ethic. No rule is 100 percent foolproof. The rule "Thou shalt not murder" is a good rule, but I for one would praise the Christian thinker Dietrich Bonhoeffer, who engaged himself in a plot to assassinate Hitler. I think I could make a case that his action was ethically justified. So rules are not perfect. But I do think that these five rules will work in the vast majority of cases and will work, with minor adjustments, equally well for men and women, gay and straight, married and unmarried.

The first rule I would propose is that sexual activity should never be coerced. No one should force another into a sexual experience. Now coercion can be of two types, I think: physical and psychological.

When someone physically coerces another person to have sex, the name for that is rape. Rape has been an extraordinarily common crime throughout much of human history, most often committed by men against women, and particularly by male soldiers against women. By most reports, rape is going on right now in 1994 in frightening numbers in the war in Eastern Europe, as well as being disturbingly common in our so-called peaceful society. It is a brutal and insensitive crime, one that we as a species need to eliminate from our spectrum of behavior. For an excellent book on the crime of rape, I heartily recommend to both men and women the book *Against Our Will* by Susan Brownmiller. It will open your eyes. A healthy ethic of sexuality condemns rape, in all of its forms, as a gross violation of the worth and dignity of a fellow human being.

The second way that sex can be coerced is by psychological means, and the way it's done is by abuse of power relationships. That is, people in stronger power positions can coerce people in weaker power positions to have sex with them. Examples of these kinds of unequal power relationships include a parent and child (or for that matter, any adult and any child), a doctor and a patient, a teacher and a student, a supervisor and an employee, a therapist and a client, or a clergy person and a counselee. All of these relationships involve one person who is stronger in the relationship and another person who, in the context of that particular relationship, is more vulnerable. Any exploitation of that inequality of power to obtain sex is coercive and unethical. Our society is overflowing with examples of this kind of coercive sexuality right now, as we become increasingly aware of the dynamics of power relationships in families and in the helping professions. People in these professions must commit themselves to an ethical standard that precludes any sexual relationship with those whom they serve. And so our ethic of sexuality rejects all forms of coerced sexual behavior.

With all of that unpleasantness out of the way, we might be tempted to say that any other sexual relationship between consenting adults is fine. From a strictly legal point of view, I might be tempted to agree. But from an ethical point of view, I think we still have more to examine. And so I will propose my second rule, which is that we all have an ethical obligation to exercise wisdom regarding the procreation of human life.

"...not only is birth control not intrinsically evil, it is an absolute moral imperative, without which the human race cannot possibly survive in anything like its present form."

Not only is population size one of the most serious problems of the human race right now, but individuals and their families, as well as our systems to meet social service needs, are strained to the limit by births that often are not planned or even wanted. All of us have an ethical obligation to take reasonable precautions not to bring children into this world if we are not prepared to care for and nurture them.

I repeat, not only is birth control not intrinsically evil, it is an absolute moral imperative, without which the human race cannot possibly survive in anything like its present form. When

God said be fruitful and multiply, there were only two people he said it to. Now there are five billion. The religious and ethical messages must change.

Third, and somewhat related to the second, is the obligation we all have to take precautions against the spread of disease through sexual activity. It seems to me that this has always been true, but of course it is particularly so these days with the reality of AIDS. Each of us has a responsibility to govern our own behavior in such a way as to minimize the possibility of transmitting AIDS or any other disease to another person. This means taking precautions such as using condoms, making a wise choice of partners, getting tested for HIV, and being honest with sexual partners about one's medical condition. AIDS is an extraordinarily devastating disease. It has achieved a status in our society roughly equivalent to the status of leprosy in biblical times. We need to de-stigmatize this disease, to see it as a medical problem, and to do everything we can in our public and private lives to make sure that it is not transmitted through sexual activity. That is the responsibility of each one of us.

The fourth general rule that I want to propose this morning is that those of us who have entered into a marriage, or any other kind of committed relationship, need to keep the agreements we have made with our partners regarding our sexuality. Most people who get married or who consciously enter into a committed relationship have an agreement, either explicit or implicit, not to become involved in sexual relationships with other persons.

This is not true for all couples, of course. When I was growing up, there was a family that lived down the street from us in which the married couple clearly had an agreement that extramarital affairs were okay, perhaps even encouraged. I knew them well enough to know that this was an open

"Any committed relationship is a challenging and sometimes fragile thing."

and, I think, basically honest agreement between them. While I do not think I would personally want to live that lifestyle, neither do I condemn it on ethical or moral grounds, as long as the other ethical guidelines are observed.

But when couples do have agreements with each other not to be sexually involved with other people, then I think they are ethically bound to keep those agreements. Any committed relationship is a challenging and sometimes fragile thing. One of the requirements for its success is trust. And trust regarding such an emotionally charged aspect of life as sexuality is, for most couples, particularly important. When that trust is broken, it can be a particularly serious situation.

It is certainly true that circumstances can change radically from the day we said "I do." What seemed like a natural thing to promise at that time may seem totally unnatural later on. What that tells us is that our relationship is in trouble; it needs to change and to grow. We may need counseling or some other kind of intervention to get it back on track. We may need to make a change in the agreement we have made with our partner. But we should make that change openly and honestly, if at all possible, and avoid the situation of violating the agreement first and then saying we need to make a change afterward.

Fortunately, many committed relationships can survive a breach of trust and may even emerge stronger after a time of healing; but of course, some relationships do not survive. What seems true to me, from an ethical standpoint, is that we human creatures need to be able to depend on each other when we make agreements and covenants with each other in virtually all aspects of life. This is no less true in the delicate area of sexuality, where feelings are especially sensitive. Therefore, let us respect our committed relationships.

Finally, and perhaps most important, I want to propose to you this morning that every sexual act in our lives— and indeed I would say every act, period—needs to be undertaken in a context of care and concern for the well-being of both ourselves and others. I know that this is not a very specific rule, but it is perhaps the most fundamental rule, the rule of love. We are at every moment called upon to act so as to nurture our own well-being and that of others.

I can't say how this rule will play out in every situation. For a teenage girl, it may mean having the self-esteem and the courage to say no when she feels uncomfortable with what she is being pressured to do. For the teenage boy she is with, it may mean having the sensitivity and genuine caring to hear that "no" and to respect and honor it.

For young people in general, the rule of care and concern, or love of self and others, would mean that we should look at how our developing sexuality affects every aspect of our lives—our self-esteem, our schoolwork, our career plans, our relationship with our parents, our health, our friendships. Then we must look for those actions that contribute most to our overall well-being and the well-being of those around us. My feeling is that for most young people still living at home, the healthy approach would be to go slow, not to jump too quickly into being sexually active. But I offer that as advice, not as condemnation.

For couples in committed relationships, the rule of love of self and others would encourage us to honor and respect our partner and to be sensitive to signs that the flow of love and intimacy is breaking down. Long-term relationships are not a simple matter. Almost every long-term relationship needs renewal at crucial times. When such a relationship feels stuck or passionless, we should not hesitate to get professional counseling.

For single adults, the rule of love of self and others would encourage us to be sensitive to our own needs and long-term goals. Are we looking for a long-term commitment? If so, are we perhaps stuck in a pattern that is self-defeating or just not fulfilling? Again, professional help may be useful if we feel stuck.

For us as a society, the rule of care and concern for self and others should push us, I think, in the direction of tolerance and respect for differences. It should also push us in the direction of encouraging the best possible choices in our society regarding sexual matters. Widespread availability of birth control, sex education, and counseling services would seem to be rather obvious steps in the right direction, and we should all work toward making these more available.

". . . the rule of care and concern for self and others should push us, I think, in the direction of tolerance and respect for differences."

I wish I could now say that I have covered all the bases, but I know there are many issues still hanging. It seems to me that some issues are pretty clear-cut: that sex should not be coerced, that heterosexuals have a responsibility to use birth control, that we all have a responsibility to take precautions against the spread of disease, and that when we enter into agreements about our sexuality with people we love, we ought to keep those agreements. Beyond those four situations that seem pretty clear-cut to me, I can only appeal to the rule of care and concern for self and others, which I believe will lead us in the right direction in the various situations of our lives, if we take it seriously.

Many ancient cultures worshipped the sexual force as divine, and in so doing, I think they had a valid intuition. Sexuality is powerful, enticing, creative, dangerous, and—at least sometimes—beyond our control. It is our task to access the power of this divine energy for the service of joy, of pleasure, of intimacy, of the creation of life itself. It will not do to simply say it is bad and avoid it, because it will keep popping out of whatever cage we put it in. Neither will it do to turn this power loose, unrestricted, to go wherever it will. That would indeed be like lighting fires all over town.

I recommend to you today a middle way, a way of both freedom and responsibility, a way that recognizes both the value of joyful abandon and the necessity of limits. This tension is a fundamental one in our lives, but one that will yield up to us a harvest of pleasure and creativity, if we can continue to face it with both playfulness and a sense of integrity. ∞

Everyone knows I'm a baseball fan and, thankfully, most folks are pretty tolerant of that fact. This sermon was given complete with a first pitch thrown down the center aisle and the congregation singing "Take Me Out to the Ball Game" as the morning hymn. The local newspaper covered the event and published an article on the sermon in the next day's sports section. — MB

A League of Our Own

October 11, 1992

My name is Michael Brown, and I am a baseball fan. I don't really know exactly how I got to be a baseball fan; I don't remember ever making a conscious decision to become a baseball fan. It just kind of happened. I do remember playing baseball as a kid, mostly in church leagues, which were pretty serious leagues for us Southern Baptists. I was a fairly good player, but certainly not outstanding. I do remember pretty clearly pitching one inning of a church league game when I was about ten or eleven. I didn't allow any runs, but I did walk two or three batters. I was glad to let someone else pitch the next inning.

I also remember rooting for the Milwaukee Braves against the New York Yankees in the '57 and '58 World Series. I also rooted for the '59 White Sox, and Luis Aparicio became one of my heroes. I had a magnificent collection of baseball cards, and to this day I don't know what became of them. I had cards like Warren Spahn, Lew

36

Burdette, Mickey Mantle, and Duke Snider. The loss of my baseball card collection still hurts to this very day.

During my teenage and early adult years, I was utterly uninterested in baseball. These were my years of rebellion. The Vietnam War was going on, and young people were into protesting and drugs. Baseball was an incredibly uncool, establishment-oriented opiate of the masses that my friends and I had no use for.

It was in my late twenties and early thirties that baseball made a comeback in my life. Perhaps it was because I was feeling ready to give America another chance. In retrospect, perhaps baseball was one American institution that seemed harmless enough and had some power to connect me with the innocence of childhood, or maybe it was the special attraction of rooting for the Cubs. I don't know why—it just happened. When my wife and I got married, I asked her as part of our marriage agreement to become a Cubs fan. She agreed, and faithfully kept the agreement for many years; however, she claims that since we don't live in Chicago anymore, she doesn't have to keep rooting for the Cubs. I think I can probably accept that modification in our marriage.

I don't know when it first occurred to me that baseball has religious or spiritual significance. It may seem like a rather preposterous idea at first

glance, but as time goes on, I am increasingly convinced that this is true. And evidently I am not
the only one. I have at least a dozen colleagues
among Unitarian Universalist ministers who agree
with me, and I served as a hospital chaplain with
a Presbyterian minister who was even more wild
about baseball than I am. And of course, a whole
bunch of recent movies have sought to explore the
more subtle, even spiritual, dimensions of baseball,
perhaps most notably *The Natural* and *Field of
Dreams*, both of which have very spiritual over-
tones. So I'm certainly not alone in this view, and I
propose here to relate to you some of my thoughts
and feelings about the game of baseball; specifically,
and in all seriousness, what I see as the spiritual and
religious dimensions of the game.

Now, I am aware that at first glance, baseball
may appear to be anything but spiritual. A bunch
of overpaid, whiny grown men standing around
spitting and scratching is not exactly the most
spiritual thing in the world. And I agree there is
much about professional sports in general, and
baseball in particular, that is objectionable. But
I would suggest to you that many aspects of life
that we hold as being meaningful are equally problematic. The whole Judeo-Christian tradition is
riddled with problems, yet this does not mean that
it has no value or truth. Our American democracy
is alarmingly corrupt and in many ways ineffective,

but the ideal of self-government is still very meaningful, to me at least. As with so many areas of life, we have to look beneath the surface, beneath the spitting and the scratching, to see what is going on in baseball.

It may also be objected that baseball is exclusively the province of males, and is therefore irrelevant for women. I do not believe this is true, although I readily admit that baseball, and indeed sports in general, is male-dominated in our culture. But the metaphor of baseball, like all the great metaphors, is pliable. It's flexible enough to accommodate many points of view, even self-critical ones. And I would submit to you that any religious metaphor worth its salt must be capable of multiple interpretations, multiple layers of meaning.

" . . . any religious metaphor worth its salt must be capable of multiple interpretations, multiple layers of meaning. "

The recent movie by Penny Marshall, *A League of Their Own*, certainly made a delightful attempt to show baseball as a women's sport. And by the way, did you know that Peoria had a women's baseball team, the Peoria Redwings, from 1946 to 1951, coached by a man named "Rawmeat Bill" Rodgers? They played in the All-American Girls Professional Baseball League, the league depicted in the movie with Madonna. So evidently, baseball can be viewed as a woman's game as well as a man's. No one could possibly watch athletes like Martina Navratilova and Kristi Yamaguchi without realizing that competitive sports can be a very serious enterprise for women.

The other objection that I want to answer right off the bat (so to speak) is that competitive sports in general are bad and should be discouraged. While I have some sympathy for this point of view, I must admit that at this point in my life, I do not feel that competition is inherently a bad thing. My sense of reality is that the life process is ordered by a kind of paradoxical arrangement involving both competition and cooperation. My limited understanding of ecological systems is that life-forms both compete and cooperate with each other to produce stable ecosystems.

I am very much of the opinion that human societies need to make enormous strides in our ability to cooperate, but I do not believe this means that competition should die out. Of all human institutions that I am aware of, perhaps the most cooperative of all is the celebration of the Olympics every four years, an organized competition. Any organized competition requires a high degree of cooperation. And so I see competition and cooperation not as mortal enemies, but as paradoxically interdependent.

So with that long preamble, I will tell you what I think is going on at baseball games symbolically, underneath the surface of the commercialism and the sometimes crude male behavior. If our western culture has two primary sources, the Judeo-Christian and the Greco-Roman, our traditions of competitive sports definitely come from the Greek and Roman side, from the pagans. They originated the idea of athletic contests as sacred festivals, religious celebrations.

The stadium is a kind of *temenos*, a Greek word that means an enclosed space set apart from the rest of the world for sacred activities. Note, by the way, how much trouble you can get into for going onto a baseball field if you are not authorized to be there, if you are uninvited. This is partly our modern obsession with security, but it is also partly a remnant of the idea of sacred space—a space for gods and heroes to play their divine games, not a space for ordinary, everyday use.

Notice that the space is divided into two kinds, fair and foul, sort of a secular version of sacred and profane. Notice also that both the fair and foul spaces extend outward infinitely. There is no end to where a fair ball can go. It can go as far as a human being

"The stadium is a kind of temenos . . . *an enclosed space set apart from the rest of the world for sacred activities . . . a space for gods and heroes to play their divine games."*

can hit it. Baseball jargon routinely refers to balls as being hit into orbit, knocked out of this world, and so on. Last night I met a man at a wedding who said, "He hit it so far that they're still looking for it."

The space enclosed by the stadium is filled with luscious green grass, an unmistakable symbol of fertility. Baseball in particular, of all the sports, follows the natural cycle of the seasons. To say that the baseball season is beginning, with all its hopes and dreams, is another way of saying that it is spring. For the baseball season to end, as it is doing now, is another way of saying that summer is over, and those of us who are fans watch our favorite teams fall into their annual defeat as the leaves fall from the trees. The cycle of nature reigns supreme. Only one team will survive; all the rest will be defeated. That one team alone will beat the odds, beat what seems like the inevitability of death, and achieve immortality. All the rest will die, only to be resurrected with new hope in the coming spring. Baseball is a game of sadness, of disappointment, but also a game of hope and new life.

". . . the two teams represent the duality of life, the inevitable conflicts and struggles we all have to go through."

I would say that the two teams represent the duality of life, the inevitable conflicts and struggles we all have to go through. But the game itself, the larger reality, represents the larger cooperative unity into which the competitive, smaller elements fit. The umpires represent the impartial, uncaring laws of the universe. We can get mad at them if we want to; they can even appear to be grossly unfair at times; but ultimately there is nothing we can do about it. They are in charge, not us. Getting mad doesn't help. You play by the rules or you're out of the game.

The role of the player is to step up to the plate and take a swing at what life throws at him or her. If our swing is successful, we are off and running, off on an adventure which may or may not be successful. The ultimate success is to return from the adventure, to arrive back home exactly where we started. But the fact that we completed the adventure in between the leaving and the returning is what makes the returning count, makes it significant. As T. S. Eliot wrote, "The end of all our exploring will be to arrive where we started and know the place for the first time." The team that most successfully cooperates in getting its players back home is the winner.

The entire enterprise is a test: a test of skill, a test of character, a test of will and strength and determination, a test of selflessness. The player who dives for the ball with no concern for personal safety may seem crazy to us, but that player has extended himself or herself, has gone beyond a limiting self-interest. It is a kind of hero journey, a quest for something very valuable. As in the classic hero journey described by Joseph Campbell, the quest is really a search for the true nature of oneself. The game becomes a path of self-knowledge, where the kinds of questions asked and answered are questions like, "What can I do if I push myself to the limit?" "What am I capable of? How will I behave under pressure?" "Will I let my fear get the best of me or will I have courage?" "How will I deal with failure, with loss? How much do I care?" "How hard am I willing to work?" "What does it mean to win or lose?"

So the players on the field of sacred space are, at least in some sense, reenacting the timeless hero myth. The competing team does us a favor by representing the challenges we have to overcome on the quest—our monsters, our dreams. At least in this particular model of reality, we need the adversary to find out who we are. Of course, the ultimate lesson taught by competition is that we really compete most deeply with our own inner selves. But we need the other team in order to find that out!

As we, the spectators, enter into the reality of the game, an unusual sense of community takes hold in our awareness and in our behavior. Due to our common affection for a team, we find that we have a kind of instant communication with people we have never met before. We laugh and joke with them and maybe even physically touch, like giving a high five or maybe performing a wave together. The wave is a very clear metaphor for community, where many act in harmony and behave as one.

Since baseball is inevitably a game of many losses, the community has ample opportunity to grieve together, and the grief at baseball games is usually more spontaneous and uninhibited than in most other social situations. Hearing 50,000 people groan together, spontaneously, unrehearsed, in perfect unison, is an amazing thing. It suggests the possibility of highly coordinated human action and response. We seem to have lost the art of communal grief. I think I have only really experienced it once, and that was when President Kennedy was assassinated. Then we as a people, a nation, all groaned together, a tragic but beautiful communal experience.*

And of course, the community of fans also celebrates together, often with ecstatic self-expression mostly unheard of in any other sphere of life: people jumping up and down, yelling, and screaming in a truly uninhibited way. People really let go at baseball games. But, you may say the game has no significance, and that is correct. The game has no significance at all. That's an essential ingredient to

*Since this sermon was written, the terrorist attacks of 9/11 became another occasion for communal grieving. —Ed.

its success as a metaphor. Its only significance is in what it reveals about us. Roger Angell, the excellent baseball writer featured in *The New Yorker,* writes, "Baseball seems to have been invented solely for the purpose of explaining all other things in life."

That is the beauty of the game for me: it is all metaphor, 100 percent. It has no utilitarian value whatsoever; it is, as they say, "just a game." If it has become an enormous social phenomenon and hugely successful business enterprise, it is because it works so well as a metaphor for the rest of life. And we are willing to consistently spend our time and money to witness and participate in that metaphor. We project our search for meaning onto the game. The virtue the game possesses is simply that it works well as a reflector of our own inner processes. I don't know why it works so well. Maybe it's something as simple as the long interval between pitches, which provides time for reflection. In any case, it does work, at least for a good many of us, as a reflector of our own search for meaning.

"The game has no significance at all. That's an essential ingredient to its success as a metaphor. Its only significance is in what it reveals about us. "

Two examples from recent movies come to mind in this regard. The first is from the movie

Parenthood, in which Steve Martin plays a father whose son appears to be having some really significant problems in life. The parents have taken him to see a psychologist and have tried everything else they can think of. Finally there is a scene in which the boy is playing the outfield for his Little League baseball team. A fly ball is hit to him, and we watch him in his attempt to catch it. The movie goes into slow motion. Why? Because the moment is so intense, so laden with meaning, that we have to slow down time to take it all in. Steve Martin is going crazy; he is actually praying, as I recall, "Lord, let him catch that ball." And when the boy actually does catch the ball, there is an explosion of celebration and joy in his family that is an event of significant healing. The young boy has been initiated. He has tasted his own ability to go beyond what he thought he could do. He has a new self-image. It is a moment of grace and transcendence and redemption.

The second scene that comes to mind for me is the climactic scene of the movie *A League of Their Own*, which was a delightful film despite its mediocre reviews. In the movie, we follow the baseball career of two sisters who end up playing on two different teams in the women's professional baseball league. And, as sometimes happens, the older sister is a much better player and has always overshadowed the younger sister, so much so that this is a major problem in the younger sister's life. In the final play of the championship game, we see the younger sister get a hit at the most crucial moment. As she rounds third and heads for home with the potential winning run, we see her older sister blocking home plate, holding the ball, ready to tag her out.

Again the camera goes into slow motion. It is a moment of incredible intensity, and we need a little time to feel the full impact of the situation. The play at the plate that we are about to witness is the whole story of the two sisters' relationship, distilled into a single event. One sister blocks the other from her full potential, her full realization of life, or so it seems. The two collide at home plate, both fall down, and then we see the ball trickle out of the older sister's hands. "Safe" is the call, and a true call it is. The younger sister has arrived safely at a new level of self-esteem, of meaning, of self-worth; she has come home to herself.

I say to you again that the game means nothing. It has no intrinsic significance. What the game does for us is to provide a mirror for seeing who we are. It gives a form to our inner struggle for meaning and transformation. It is not necessarily an ideal form; it may even be seriously flawed. But if we watch closely, it can still perform acts of self-revelation for us.

I suggest to you that we human beings have a real need for forms of behavior and self-expression that can serve to reveal our hidden potential to ourselves. We need forms in which to act out the search for answers to our inner questions. We need places and spaces where we can find out who we are, what we are made of, and what we can accomplish if we really go full out. We need history, rituals, heroes and heroines. If the sports event is to mean anything at all, it must be as an inspiration for us not to remain spectators of the game of life, but to join a team and take our turn at bat.

"I suggest to you that we human beings have a real need for forms of behavior and self-expression that can serve to reveal our hidden potential to ourselves."

I invite you to find that kind of sacred arena in your life: a place—perhaps here in this church, perhaps somewhere else—where you can swing for the fences, where you can find out what you're made of, and where you can discover for yourself what deep and profound undiscovered resources exist within you. For me, this church is such a sacred space. I hope it is for you, too, or that you have another place that works for you on that level.

Even if we strike out, we will feel better for the attempt. For one of the great truths of baseball is that there is always next inning, next game, next year; there is always tomorrow, when we can try our hand one more time at the great adventure of life.

I'll see you at the ballpark, wherever that may be. ∞

Believe it or not, this and the next sermon grew out of a long-range planning process that we undertook at church. One idea came up during my research that became a real 'Aha!' for me, and this sermon and the one that follows it are the result.—MB

Taoist Wisdom and Polarity Thinking

February 6, 2000

For quite a few years now, I have been wrestling with a tension between two different ways of looking at the world, ways which appear to be irreconcilable. One of my deepest impulses is to want to improve the way things are—to right wrongs, to alleviate suffering, to fight the good fight, to stand up for justice and for freedom and against oppression, tyranny, and evil. Who could argue with those ideals?

And yet I find within myself another impulse as well. And this impulse says that the world is just fine the way it is. It doesn't need me to fix it, nor am I really capable of doing so. The world is a beautiful, amazing, and endlessly delightful place whose internal order and structure are far beyond my puny capacity to modify, let alone improve. This impulse tells me that my main job is to praise what is, to enjoy the beauty all around me, to celebrate and appreciate the world.

These two impulses that I find within me certainly appear to be at odds with one another. If the world is basically wonderful just the way it is, it certainly doesn't need me to fix it. But if there is so much that seems wrong and in need of improvement, how can the world be such a perfect place?

Our Western style of thinking, based as it is on the principle of noncontradiction, doesn't seem to point to any obvious, clear-cut way out of this dilemma. It seems as if we have to choose one or the other. And yet I, for one, cannot seem to cut either of these impulses out of my life.

Some of the Eastern philosophies, especially Taoism, are much more tolerant of paradox and contradiction than we are, even pointing to it positively as a way to the truth. Taoism in particular sees the world as the interplay of opposite tendencies, symbolized in the familiar symbol showing yin and yang fitting together to make a circle that symbolizes the wholeness of the Tao, the wholeness of life. This symbol has become almost a cliché in our culture, and yet we probably do not have a very deep sense of its real meaning.

One person who has substantially developed this idea of the relationship of apparent opposites is Roy Oswald, a senior consultant at the Alban Institute. Oswald names this way of looking at things "polarity thinking." So what is a polarity? Oswald says that a polarity is an unsolvable yet unavoidable problem that needs to be managed, not solved. Our only real options are to manage the polarity well or to manage it poorly.

So every polarity is a kind of tension between two sides, or we might say two poles. Oswald says that each of the two poles has both positive attributes and negative attributes. Let's look at an example to see how this polarity might work. One of the examples that Oswald uses is the relationship between humility and self-esteem. At first glance, these two may appear to be contradictory. Self-esteem is about thinking highly of oneself, while humility is viewing oneself in a lowly way. Oswald would say that each side of the polarity has both a positive and a negative aspect. The positive side of self-esteem is having the capacity to honor or value yourself. But when we overemphasize self-esteem, we can get caught in its negative side, which is called grandiosity or inflation—"I am the greatest thing in the world."

". . . a polarity is an unsolvable yet unavoidable problem that needs to be managed, not solved. Our only real options are to manage the polarity well or to manage it poorly."

Now here comes the interesting part. The negative side of self-esteem, namely grandiosity, is corrected by the positive side of the other pole, which is humility, or freedom from self-aggrandizement and self-involvement. But if we go overboard on humility, we can fall into self-deprecation to the point of thinking we are no good or worthless.

"A polarity is a tension that cannot be fixed. It's built into the nature of things. The only cure for a polarity is wisdom . . ."

Amazingly enough, this negative aspect of humility is again corrected by the positive side of self-esteem, namely valuing ourselves.

So here we have a polarity: two seemingly opposite values, each with positive and negative dimensions, and each value linked to the other in such a way that the negative side of each is compensated for or corrected by the positive side of the other pole. Oswald says, and I agree, that this is not a problem to be solved—in fact, it can't be solved. It is a reality to be lived; it's a tension to be managed in daily living. Wisdom is managing it well, and foolishness is failing to recognize and manage the polarity. A polarity is a tension that cannot be fixed. It's built into the nature of things. The only cure for a polarity is wisdom—learning to balance and integrate the poles of the polarity and seeing the larger wholeness within which these apparent opposites exist.

What might be some other examples of polarities in life? Let's try activity and rest. The positive side of activity has to do with energy, engagement, and accomplishment. And yet many of us know that it is possible to overengage in activity so that activity becomes exhaustion, overcommitment, and burnout. This negative side of activity, fortunately, can be corrected by the positive side of rest, which is refreshment, rejuvenation, and reinvigoration. But if rest goes unchecked, it falls into its negative side, which is laziness, lethargy, and boredom. What corrects this problem? The positive side of activity. So again, it seems like we have a polarity. Poetically, we might say that by resting we accomplish everything or that by trying to do everything we accomplish nothing, and it is these kinds of paradoxical expressions that the Tao Te Ching is full of.

The way of looking at life that is called Taoism suggests to us that polarities are a basic building block—perhaps *the* basic building block upon which reality is constructed. Reality, then, is an interlocking pattern of seemingly opposite tendencies that are actually interdependent and complementary. The wise person recognizes this profound reality and cultivates wisdom, the capacity to manage the opposites so as to enjoy the fullness of life, which is also the emptiness of life. That's the program from the Taoist point of view.

What might be some of these other polarities in life? I suspect we could make a very long list if we gave it a try. How about change and stability? How about orderliness and spontaneity? How about the cycles of nature, the rhythms of life? Winter and summer, day and night, life and death? I suspect we could fit these all into the same pattern. How about masculine and feminine? Do these somehow each need the positive aspects of the other for balance in life? I, for one, suspect that it's true. I invite you to play around with this idea and add to the list yourself.

How about good and evil? There's a tough case, if there ever was one. The Tao Te Ching says, "When people see some things as good, other things become bad." We in the West are very firmly anchored in this good-and-evil kind of thinking, but there may be other ways to look at this particular polarity.

Consider Tom Sawyer and his cousin Sid. Sid is a goody-goody. He does everything Aunt Polly wants him to. A little angel. But what a whiny bore! Whereas Tom is in many ways a bad boy. But he is also exciting, adventurous, and vibrant with the energy of life. So how do we evaluate good and bad in such a case? Polarity thinking might work. There might be such a thing as *too* good, and what would that mean? It might mean someone like Sid or the Church Lady on *Saturday Night Live*. Too bad is, unfortunately, not at all difficult to imagine. We've all seen plenty of that. We may have a polarity like this going on in our culture right now, with the "too good" religious right on one pole and a totally self-absorbed, materialistic, nihilistic decadence on the other. These would both be the negative aspects of their respective poles. I'll leave it to you to decide how well the model works. Maybe Pat Robertson needs to learn how to boogie, and people like Larry Flynt need to take seriously the ethical issues of sexual exploitation.

It's important to realize that for Taoism, the pairs of apparent opposites are not the ultimate or final truth of the way things are. The ultimate truth is the Tao, a level of integration and unity that holds the opposites together in wholeness. The deepest level of wisdom is not simply skill in managing the opposites, but rather the ability to perceive, to see the Tao, the wholeness of life. That is the very deepest level of wisdom, and it's from that level that the greatest skill in dealing with opposites emerges.

"The deepest level of wisdom is not simply skill in managing the opposites, but rather the ability to perceive, to see the Tao, the wholeness of life. That is the very deepest level of wisdom . . ."

Let me now return for just a moment to the dilemma I started out with, the two impulses I personally feel in my life: the impulse to fix the world, or at least some little piece of it, and the apparently opposite impulse to enjoy and praise the world the way it is. Perhaps these two impulses form a polarity as well. Too much activism may leave us cynical, hopeless, and burned out. But the cure for that is to drink in the wonder of life, to climb a mountain or watch a sunset or read great poetry. On the other hand, the celebratory pole may degenerate into self-absorption, insensitivity, or lack of compassion, which impels us back into the world of engagement and involvement. Both poles, tempered with wisdom, are clearly good. There is no choice to make between the two—the only choice is to manage the balance well.

"Both poles . . . are clearly good. There is no choice to make between the two— the only choice is to manage the balance well."

Interestingly enough, the Taoist view is, paradoxically, more oriented toward the pole of "appreciating the way it is," as is most Eastern religion, while Western religion is more activism- and change-oriented, the fix-it pole. Could it be that both are right, or at least exist in some kind of wise balance? This would mean that Taoism is also self-referential—that is, it provides a commentary on itself. It provides a model for putting itself in the context of a polarity. What an intriguing paradox! One could, I think, develop a taste for such fruitful paradox, as one might enjoy a fine wine.

I will tell you this: when I personally feel confused in life, the Tao Te Ching is often the scripture I turn to for a path out of the confusion. It shows us a way, which is what Tao means—a way to see what may have appeared to be crazy in a new light, a way to both celebrate what is and yet work for change. In fact, it tells us that when we look deep down into the profound wholeness of life, its deep unity and aesthetic perfection, it is precisely at that moment that we will have the best chance to make our small contributions to its amazing beauty. ⌒⌒

*Here is a second result of the 'Aha!' experience I had
while thinking about polarities. Good and evil are one of
the best known of all pairs of opposites. Could they be can-
didates for polarity thinking as well? That got me started
on this sermon. —MB*

A Polarity Theory of
Good and Evil

February 20, 2000

*The Tao doesn't take sides;
It gives birth to both good and evil.
The Master doesn't take sides;
She welcomes both saints and sinners.*

*The Tao is like a bellows:
It is empty yet infinitely capable.
The more you use it, the more it produces;
The more you talk of it, the less you un-
    derstand.*

Hold on to the center.

—*Tao Te Ching (translation by Stephen Mitchell)*

In an earlier sermon I spoke about a way
of looking at certain life issues called
polarity thinking. I first got this idea
from a man named Roy Oswald, who is a senior
consultant at the Alban Institute, an organization
that studies the behavior of religious communities.
Oswald says that a polarity is a problem that can

never really be solved; it can only be managed. Let me give you an example.

Let us consider the two different states of life called rest and activity. Rest and activity are two very different things. In some ways, they are complete opposites. One does not rest when one is active, and one lets go of activity in order to rest. And yet it's just as true that rest and activity both have positive value and work together cooperatively. We need both rest and activity to have a truly healthy life. So rest and activity do not appear to be like good and evil; on the contrary, they both certainly appear to be good.

Oswald would call such a relationship a polarity. In a polarity, both sides are good: we do not need to affirm one and condemn the other. But it's also true that both sides of the polarity have the potential to become unhealthy if carried to an extreme. So, for example, rest carried to an extreme might become laziness, stagnation, or listlessness, and activity pushed to its extreme might become overcommitment, exhaustion, or workaholism. So each side of the polarity is good, yet either side can become destructive if pushed too far. Such is the nature of polarities.

Now, another fascinating feature of polarities is that the cure for the negative or shadow aspect of one side of the polarity is the positive aspect of the other. So, for example, the cure for laziness is activity, and the cure for exhaustion is rest. The positive value of each side cures the negative part of the other side. What an interesting relationship between apparent opposites. So now you have the idea of a polarity.

Wisdom, then, is the ability to manage the polarity well, to know when each side of the polarity is called for and to avoid falling into the negative dimension of either of the two sides. The polarity is not a problem to be solved; neither side ever wins. The polarity is a reality to be lived, wisely if at all possible.

There are all kinds of polarities we might explore, but perhaps one of the most difficult, intriguing, and important sets of opposites in our cultural heritage is the set of opposites known as good and evil. Now there is a serious opposition—so serious that for many folks in our culture, the conflict between good and evil is thought of as the deepest level of truth in our human lives. It's the ultimate level of reality. So good and evil are a pretty serious business in our culture.

It is overwhelmingly tempting to consider the possibility that good and evil might be some kind of polarity, and that possibility has been intriguing me ever since I first spoke on the topic of polarities. So let's explore that idea for just a moment. If good and evil are two sides of a polarity, then we would be in the truly unusual position of talking about the bad side of good and the good side of bad, a very strange kind of talk indeed. Maybe someone out there will have the ingenuity to lay that one out. But as I continued to reflect on this good and evil business, I happened to think of a different approach that seems more promising, and I want to share my thoughts on that other approach with you today.

The approach that seems more promising to me begins with a basic idea of Sigmund Freud's, which does seem to me to fit well into the model of a polarity. Freud believed that within each person there is an unconscious dimension of the personality that he called the id, which just means the "it." This id, or "it," is a reservoir of instincts and desires that come to us as a result of our long evolutionary history—desires for food and sex and power and so on. They form a kind of basic energy drive that is essentially amoral. The id part just wants what it wants; it doesn't much care about the niceties of manners or human civilization, and therein lies the problem. Because, as everyone knows, we can't just do anything we want any time we want. We can't just hit anybody we want to hit anytime we feel like it,

"... the id, which just means the 'it' ... is a reservoir of instincts and desires that come to us as a result of our long evolutionary history ..."

or have sex with anybody we want to whenever the fancy strikes us.

The reality is that in order for human beings to live together with even a relative amount of peace, there have to be rules; there have to be limits on behavior. That's what civilization is all about, and that's what morality is all about. And so there's a tension between the mostly unconscious demands of our own inner nature and the demands of living together in a civilized society, which prevents us from acting on all of these deep desires. And this tension never really goes away, according to Freud. It's something we just have to adjust to, something we have to live with. The outlook, from Freud's point of view, never really seems to be terribly hopeful; we are more or less destined to a life of frustration between these two kinds of demands, although there are techniques, like sublimation, that help to relieve that tension.

Freud's protégé, Carl Jung, eventually broke with his teacher over the issue of the nature of the unconscious. Whereas Freud's view of the unconscious seems rather negative, Jung believed that the unconscious is a source of positive values as well, even spiritual values. It's a source of creativity and growth. What Freud called the id, Jung re-envisioned as the libido. The libido includes the primitive drives that Freud outlined, but extends beyond that dimension as well. It's the life force, the energy of the unconscious dimension of life that is constantly pushing us to grow, to expand, to realize the fullness of life.

I have tried to capture these two sets of ideas as well as I can in a polarity format in the chart on the next page. This chart is a work in progress, but I have at least provisionally named the two sides, or poles, of the polarity morality and primal energy.

"The positive side of our primal energy is creativity, spontaneity, fun, ecstasy . . . passion, imagination, and joy. But . . . it can become destructive."

The primal energy side encompasses all of those dimensions of our lives that are wild, that are natural, that are exuberant and physical and spontaneous. It's Freud's id and Jung's libido. It's the life force, biologically programmed in us as creatures. It's energy, desire, passion, sexuality, and sex appeal. It's dancing and drumming. It's laughing and having fun. It's Miller time.

The other pole is morality—the rules, the limits, the laws. It's civilization; it's conformity. It's the rules that make it possible for us to live together in peace, or at least something approaching peace. It's reason and order; it's duty and hard work and self-denial.

A Model for Pondering Issues of Good and Evil

Morality	*Primal Energy*
Civilization	Wildness, Nature
Law, Rules	Spontaneity
Limits on Behavior	Expressiveness
Superego	Id, Libido, Life Force
Responsibility	Freedom
Adult Reality	Kid Reality
Conformity	Carefree Abandon
Order	Ecstasy, Joy, Eros
Rights of Others	Desire, Passion
Manners, Politeness	Creativity, Energy
Common Good	Sexuality, Sex Appeal
Reason, Logos	Imagination, Intuition
Social Conventions	Fun, Play, Laughter
Religion	Spirituality, Sensuality
Duty, Work	Breaking the Rules
Tradition, Commitment	Physical Exuberance
Purity	Appetite, Zest for Living
Discipline	Adventure, Excitement
+	**+**
—	**—**
Self-righteousness	Violence
Tyranny, Intolerance	Destructive Sexuality
Repression, Oppression	Anarchy, Chaos
Police Brutality	Selfishness
Disregard for the Rights of Others	Disregard for the Rights of Others
Witch Hunts, Hypocrisy	Riot, Rape, Pillage
Control, Domination	Addiction
Shaming, Criticism	Boundary Violations
Burnout, Depression	Criminal Behavior
E.g. The Inquisition, Church Lady, Fundamentalism	E.g. Pirates, Marauders, Robber Barons

Now if these two poles form a polarity, as I am suggesting, then each pole has both a positive and a negative aspect. The positive side of our primal energy is creativity, spontaneity, fun, ecstasy, fulfilling and loving sexuality, passion, imagination, and joy. But if this primal energy goes totally without limits, it can become destructive. It can become violence; it can become inappropriate and destructive sexual acting out; it can become anarchy and chaos; it can become wild bands of marauders laying waste to villages, killing, raping, and burning. We have all seen those movies.

But morality has a negative side as well. In addition to the healthy aspects of morality that enable us to live together in peace, there can be such a thing as destructive or out-of-control morality. That's what self-righteousness is all about. That's what tyranny and oppression are all about. That's what police brutality is all about. Morality is about being right, but when some people get the idea that their ideas are the only right ones, they can easily slip into intolerance and oppression. A lighthearted example of this is the Church Lady character on *Saturday Night Live*. But for me, the Inquisition would be the all-time example of how this shadow side of morality can emerge. The good guys quite literally morphed into the bad guys by trying to impose their standards of morality and righteousness onto others, and in so doing they fell into an unbelievable, blood-curdling level of evil.

So both sides have both positive and negative dimensions. And if this is a polarity, we should be able to find the cure for the negative side of each pole in the positive side of the other. I would propose that we can do just that. It is pretty clear that the correction for the out-of-control primal energy of the lower right quadrant is the positive side of morality. And I would suggest that the antidote to the oppressiveness of the negative, tyrannical side of morality is freedom and self-expression, which are parts of the positive side of primal energy. Freedom is always the cry in times of oppression, and creativity and self-expression are a common way to protest against oppression. That's what happened in America in the 1960s. So I believe that this pair of values does form a polarity.

Now—how about good and evil? Where do they fit in? I would propose that the healthiest way to live is to affirm the positive sides of both morality and primal energy and to avoid falling into either of the negative sides. We might then call the top half of the chart good and the bottom half evil. That's one possibility. And if we're going to continue to use the words good and evil, then I would propose that this is the best way to do so.

But let me just explore with you for a moment what I think our cultural situation is, because this is not how our culture does it. To do this, I want to reflect on one of the most significant stories of our culture, the story of Adam and Eve in the Garden of Eden. I am going to propose what may seem like a strange interpretation of that story to you, but I think it may have value.

You all know how the story goes. God creates Adam and Eve and gives them the garden to tend, with the rule being that they may not eat the fruit of one specific tree. But the serpent tempts them and they disobey, bringing about the complex of tragic consequences known as the Fall.

I want to propose that in the story of the Garden, the character of God stands for the morality side of the polarity, and the primal energy side of the polarity is symbolically represented by the serpent. If that's true, then from a polarity point of view, they both represent positive values. God represents the positive side of morality, and the serpent represents the positive side of amoral nature—desire and sexuality and enjoyment of life. Please note that we are now saying that these are good things that the serpent represents. And indeed, in ancient times the serpent was a positive symbol of life and also of the goddess. In ancient times the serpent was the symbol of another kind of religion often called fertility religion.

But as you all know, the way we know the story today is that God is good and the serpent is bad. And symbolically, what that says about us is that culturally, and especially in Christianity from about the fourth century on, the whole right-hand side of the polarity—the whole primal energy side, top and bottom, positive and negative, the side of nature and our physical bodies—got to be declared evil. That's what the story says, and that is, culturally, what has happened.

And that, by the way, is how sexuality got to be classified as evil as well. And in so doing, our culture created a serious split in our collective psyches. We split off a huge piece of who we are and called it evil. And I can't think of any better way to describe the devastating effect of that split than by using the image of being kicked out of the Garden, being kicked out of paradise, being kicked out of the good life. What a devastating moment.

". . . culturally, and especially in Christianity from about the fourth century on, the whole right-hand side of the polarity . . . the side of nature and our physical bodies— got to be declared evil. "

And as if this weren't bad enough, as a by-product of this demonizing of the primal energy of life, we have also, or at least some of us have, made the whole left-hand side, the morality side, good—even the negative aspect of morality. This would explain how religion can become oppressive, as happens all too often. It

70

happens when religion demonizes the whole right hand side of the polarity, including nature, sexuality and physical bodies, while at the same time sanctioning the whole left hand side, even the shadow part, including oppression, intolerance, tyranny and an attitude of domination toward the environment. What a mess! What is there to be done?

I want to suggest two possible shifts in our thinking that can help to heal some of these wounds. One of them is to shift the good and evil balance back to where it belongs, using the polarity model. That means affirming the primal energy of life, affirming freedom and creativity and spontaneity and even sexuality as good gifts, some of the best life has to offer—the path to joy. But it also means acknowledging the moral dimension as well, that the primal energy has to be channeled into ways that allow us to live in peace, free from the fear of being physically or psychologically violated. Both sides are true; both are important. Neither can be bargained away. It also means speaking out when either side becomes destructive, even if it's the supposed guardians of righteousness who are off the mark.

The other shift is to remember that in this old, old story, there is something called the Garden. What is the Garden? It's the place where, at least for a while, God and the serpent, Adam and Eve, all found a good life together before we split ourselves apart. It's the symbol of hope! It says that a reconciliation is possible, that the eternal conflict of opposites is not the only story in town. There is a prior reality, and therefore a deeper reality, called the Garden, or the Tao—or enlightenment or reconciliation or whatever name you like—where the opposites not only coexist but actually complement each other. That is the place we want to go; that is the way we want to live, the way of wholeness. We might not ever totally get there—we may always feel the tension of the opposites—but we can live lives that move in that direction, lives of wisdom. And if we do, then life will become progressively more joyful, more fulfilling, and more worthy to be called truly good. It will indeed become, as the old song says, "the valley of love and delight."

I had planned to preach on a totally different topic this week, but during discussion in our Adult Religious Education class a few nights before, this particular image hit me so intensely that I scrapped my planned sermon. This is what came out. —MB

The Ego and the Earth

February 6, 1994

I am determined not to spend our time together telling you about all the environmental problems we have in order to convince you that we earth inhabitants have a significant crisis on our hands. It seems to me that, for the most part, people already have that information. What we really need to hear at this point are some suggestions on how we can begin finding solutions.

When I was in Chicago in 1993 attending the Parliament of the World's Religions, I was deeply impressed by the presentation made by Gerald Barney, author of *The Global 2000 Report Revisited*. Dr. Barney made a very simple, straightforward case—that we're already well along the road of two highly significant trends: the rapid and accelerating growth of human population and, simultaneously, the startling decline of a whole range of resources our population uses to fuel our lifestyle on this planet—resources like fossil fuel, rain forests, diversity of species, arable land, and so

73

on. The combination of mushrooming population and shrinking resources adds up to a rather bleak picture of the likely future of human life on earth.

On this occasion, Gerald Barney stood before some two to three thousand religious leaders of the world and said, in all seriousness, that in its essence this is a spiritual problem—not a technical or an economic problem primarily, but a spiritual one. I would like here to try to put my finger on what he meant by this statement.

I think his meaning was that we already have the technology available to solve the challenges of the environmental crisis. All of the knowledge, or at least a vast amount of it, already exists. We know how to lower population growth by means of birth control. We know how to stop cutting down rain forests. We know how to stop producing chemicals that deplete the ozone. We have some knowledge of how to use less fossil fuel. We know how to distribute food to starving people: trucks have been invented, and they can be filled with food and driven to where it's needed.

What we do not have is the collective will to do these things. You and I might have that will as individuals—or we may think that we do—but collectively, as a species, we don't have anything remotely close to that kind of committed will. That lack of a communal will, that lack of any commonly held set of values that would motivate us all to address these issues while we still have a chance, is what I think Gerald Barney is referring to when he says this is fundamentally a spiritual problem. I think he's right in his assessment.

I take Gerald Barney seriously in his challenge to religious people of all persuasions on this earth to search the wisdom of the world to find some spiritual insight that would shed light on this crisis, a crisis that threatens the very survival of our human civilization.

". . . we already have the technology available to solve the challenges of the environmental crisis. . . . What we do not have is the collective will to do these things."

In searching the various traditions I am familiar with, I am struck by a particular line of thought that will require us to take off on a tangent for a little while into a discussion of Jungian psychology. So I'll ask you to bear with me while I put on the table a few ideas that may seem, at first glance, to have absolutely nothing to do with environmental problems. I promise to tie it all together at the last.

So here goes our detour into Jungian psychology.

I once gave a sermon entitled "Ego and Self," which some of you may have heard. The basic idea of that sermon is that in Jungian psychology there are two very different ways to talk about personal identity, about who we are, who I am. Actually, there are probably more than two, but we'll stick to these two for now.

The first way is to talk about the aspect of ourselves that Jung calls the *ego*. The ego is our conscious self, our conscious personality, the part of who we are that we normally think of as "I" when we say "I want," "I am," "I think," "I act," and so on. That "I" is called the ego.

"From a Jungian point of view, our developmental journey through life can be described as a sequence of different relationships between ego and self."

Jung, like almost every other respected psychologist, believes that this ego is not all of who we are. There is a lot of who we are, a lot of our psyche, that is unconscious. I think most of us in this day and age pretty much take for granted the existence of the unconscious; but if you still feel skeptical about it, I think, given enough time, I could convince you that the unconscious does exist — that it is very real.

How would I do that? I would talk to you about your dreams, those little nightly messages from the unconscious. I would talk to you about how advertising works. I would talk to you about literature and mythology. If all of that failed, I would ask you why you fell in love with the person or persons that you did fall in love with. We could pursue that line of investigation for a while. But for now I'm going to assume you're convinced that a significant portion of each of our psyches, yours and mine, is, in fact, unconscious.

The word that Jung uses to describe the totality of the psyche, both conscious and unconscious together, is the *self*. So we have these two different notions of identity: the ego, or the conscious identity, and the self, which is the totality of both conscious and unconscious elements. From a Jungian point of view, our developmental journey through life can be described as a sequence of different relationships between ego and self.

When a baby is in the works, and even after it is born, it is almost purely self. It does not have an awareness of itself as a separate entity. It does not have a separate ego. It is mostly unconscious, utterly unconcerned with the impression it makes and the rules of human etiquette. I think that is partly what makes new babies so appealing to us, but that's another matter.

As we grow up, especially in the first half of life, we work hard to develop our egos, our separate, unique identities as differentiated from those of our parents and peers; but in doing so we also cut ourselves off from that larger unconscious self, that feeling of wholeness and naturalness. The process eventually creates in us a feeling of alienation, which can produce what is often called the midlife crisis, a time when we feel a strong urge to go off and "find ourselves." People in this strange state often go off and do unexpected things, like changing careers to a totally new field.

"*Jung once said that for people over 40, the cure for any neurosis almost always involves a spiritual transformation of some sort . . . some form of subordination of the ego to the self . . .*"

From a Jungian point of view, the second half of life is basically about rediscovering the self, a sense of wholeness and integration, or a sense of being part of a larger reality beyond just our individual ego. Interestingly enough, people who appear to be discovering that larger self often refer to the way they feel as a kind of second childhood or innocence. Jung believed that this search for the self—or *individuation*, as he called it—is, in its essence, a religious, or perhaps I should say spiritual, enterprise.

Jung once said that for people over 40, the cure for any neurosis almost always involves a spiritual transformation of some sort. The essence of this spiritual transformation is, almost without exception, some form of subordination of the ego to the self, some sort of surrender of ego, which results in realization of a larger, freer sense of aliveness and health. I would suggest to you that this principle is true in virtually every religious tradition, including religious humanism.

Jungians are very much enamored of using religious symbolism to show how this principle works. For example, looking at the myth of the Garden of Eden as a symbolic representation of the changes in the ego/self relationship, we would say that the character God represents the self, whereas Adam and Eve are both ego figures, Adam for a man and Eve for a woman. The Garden before the Fall represents the infant state, in which the self rules and all is in perfect harmony. The disobedience of God's law represents the separation of ego and self that must occur if we are to develop as individuals.

There is a loss and pain in that separation. We lose the Garden, that sense of wholeness, and there is a sense in which all of the rest of life is about trying to get that wholeness back. In the Judeo-Christian tradition, it is Jesus who shows us how to do that. The way he does it is to surrender his own ego to the will of the Father who, I would remind you, represents the self. That is what the symbol of the crucifixion is all about. Not my will but thy will be done, it says symbolically. This is the ego surrendering to the self. In that surrender, the Garden is regained under a new name: heaven. When I was a kid, I was taught that hell is separation from God, and heaven is being with God. Symbolically, that says that the separation of ego and self brings suffering, and the surrendering of ego to self brings joy and happiness.

I know this has been a long detour, but one more step and we're finished. In the Jungian framework, one of the dangers that we must face in the ego/self relationship is called *inflation*. Inflation is the state in which the ego believes that it is the self; it usurps the role of the self. Inflation is thinking that you are God. Some of our TV evangelists may sometimes seem to be in this state of inflation. They think they're God, or perhaps just God's very special messenger.

Many of the Greek tragedies are about inflation. The story of Agamemnon perhaps is one of the most well known. Agamemnon returns home from the Trojan War and is lured by his very angry wife to step on the purple carpet as he disembarks. In Greek symbolism, that purple carpet is reserved for the gods, and by stepping on it, Agamemnon is saying that he is a god. That is inflation, or *hubris*, as the Greeks called it. Inflation always comes before a fall, and sure enough, Agamemnon is soon dead, a victim of his own hubris. The only cure for inflation is to restore the right relationship between ego and self, where self is acknowledged as higher and ego is devoted to service to that self. "Not my will but Thy will be done, oh Lord."

Now, I would like to offer you an analogy that has two parts. The first part is that in our current environmental crisis, the relationship of human beings to the earth is like the relationship of the ego to the self. Second, and more specifically, at this point in history the relationship of human beings to the earth is the relationship of *inflated* ego to the self. Let me try to draw out that analogy in a little more detail.

First, let us look at the analogy of human beings as a sort of ego component of the whole earth system. We have come out of a vast and ancient natural process in which our ancestors, at least by some measurements, were far less conscious of self than we are now. Now we alone have developed this phenomenon of self-awareness, which was a giant developmental step to be sure, but also a painful one. And it has caused a sense of separateness, of alienation between ourselves and the rest of the natural world.

The natural world around us functions in this analogy something like Jung's collective unconscious functions for our individual egos. Just as it says in Genesis, we had to leave the garden

> "... we have had a special role to play in the natural process. We are the 'I' of that process ... We, collectively as a species, are the ego of the earth."

of unconscious wholeness when we developed self-awareness. But we have had a special role to play in the natural process, that of being the part of the process that had this special awareness. We are the ego of the system. As the physicist Wheeler said, "A human being is an atom's way of being aware of itself." We are that part of this natural process most able to consciously direct the process, to build, to mold, to change, to create, to destroy. We are the "I" of that process. We, collectively as a species, are the ego of the earth.

Now, I want to explore for just a moment that second part of the analogy, which says that at this crucial point in our development we are in the problematic relationship of an inflated ego to the larger self of the earth. We are walking on the forbidden purple carpet because we have committed the grievous error of inflation, of hubris. We have believed in our hearts and acted with our bodies as if we, the humans, in fact run the show, as if we were the supreme command center for the processes of nature. As our former minister, David Maynard, was quoted in *Time* magazine as saying, "The moral challenge in genetic research is not the discoveries of science, but human hubris that man can outwit nature. Only when we see ourselves as responsible parts of the chain of all life will the 'right' choices be made."

We are in that inflated position in which the ego (in this analogy, humankind) thinks it is the self, the ruler of nature. We know from psychology and from mythology that the next thing that usually happens is that the character with the inflated ego is brought low—usually killed, but sometimes only maimed. My judgment is that we as humans are in that time slot when we are still enjoying the walk on the carpet, but that enjoyment is destined to be short-lived. The true rulers of the universe—it doesn't really matter what you call them, Yahweh, Kali, the Greek gods, or the laws of nature—are about to dispense to us the inevitable consequences of our inflation. They are going to show us, in no uncertain terms, who is really running the show so that we will get the message. And it will not be a pretty sight when they do.

"Only when we see ourselves as responsible parts of the chain of all life will the 'right' choices be made."

Gerald Barney and many other scientists believe that there is a window of opportunity, that we still have to reorient ourselves (an interesting phrase) and avoid major tragedy. But, he says, the problem is a spiritual one, and he asks the religious leaders of the world to come up with a solution. And if the analogy I have suggested today is anywhere nearly on track, he is right to make that request.

What would a solution look like? What kind of changes would it involve? If this analogy is worth anything at all, then we ought to be able to transfer some of the insights of religion and psychology regarding the ego/self relationship back into the environmental sphere and have the suggestion of some answers. What would those answers look like?

"I think the first insight this line of thought would suggest to us is that we, the human species, need to acknowledge collectively that we do not run the universe. . . . We are the creatures, not the gods."

I think the first insight this line of thought would suggest to us is that we, the human species, need to acknowledge collectively that we do not run the universe. We did not invent gravity. We did not create the life process. We did not jump-start evolution. On the contrary, we are the products, the offspring, of those forces—those gods, if you will. We are the creatures, not the gods.

The inflated ego, to be cured, must recognize a power higher than itself. And I would suggest that whether you think of yourself as a theist or a nontheist, we all live in the presence of some mysterious power that has created us. It may have been intentional or not, it may have been by design or by accident; it doesn't really matter at this moment. Either way, *It* is more powerful than we are.

I think that's why some of us at certain times in our lives have had such significant experiences in the wilderness. We had an experience of the primal power of the universe, of the larger reality of which we are only a part. Far from being a downer for us, this realization is actually a source of enormous joy. We experience, in a way, our deeper self; the trees and birds and snakes and mountains are part of ourselves. Every great religious tradition has taught that great truth.

So the transformation that we as a species stand in need of is, first, to recognize the natural world as, in fact, our own larger self. And second, we need to make a conscious decision to surrender to it, to become disciples of its greater wisdom. We need to say to the natural world, "Not our human will be done, but thy natural will be done." Or as Chief Seattle put it more poetically in his famous words, "The earth does not belong to us, we belong to the earth."

You may say there's not very much likelihood of that happening, and perhaps you're right. But if it is to happen, or if anything remotely close to that is going to happen, then I think Gerald Barney is right that the religious of the world will have to become players in the process. Because it is in the world's religions that the images and symbols already exist which can restore humanity to a right relationship with nature. As a matter of fact, all the symbols are present, but they will need to be reinterpreted with an ecological perspective.

Specifically, I believe what has traditionally been thought of as an external being called God will need to be reinterpreted as qualities present in the natural world. This very change has been one of the contributions of feminist theology, which honors the earth as divine, as sacred. In theological language, we are talking about a shift from thinking of God as transcendent, or *out there somewhere*, to God as immanent, God as present in the grass and trees and creatures of the earth.

I hope each of us will be able to play an important role in that reinterpretation, and that the religions of the world will respond to Gerald Barney's challenge to come up with those reinterpreted symbols and teach them to every child and adult on earth. We need a common vision with the kind of sanctity that only the world's religions could give to it. Then we may be able to return to the simple wisdom of seeing the Garden of Eden as a real, possible garden on this earth, one that we may still be exiled from, but one that we deeply and urgently need to return to, and one that is still calling to us to come back home. ⟳

I kept seeing a particular TV commercial that showed the weekend warrior with all his paraphernalia out attacking the forces of nature, and I just had to testify.
—*MB*

The Sermon on the Lawn

I am not here to give anyone direct advice on lawn care; I can't even figure out what to do with my own lawn. I'm not particularly good at gardening. Those of you who know how to grow flowers and bushes and vegetables, you are people I regard as almost like shamans, people with precious knowledge. I have no particular knowledge to impart on any of these subjects. In fact, I myself am eager to learn.

We all have to ask ourselves in this life what it is that we're good at, what are our talents, what are our gifts; and I personally have come to the conclusion that, whatever gifts I might have, near the top of that list would be the art of interpreting symbols. That's one thing I definitely have an interest in and perhaps some talent for.

So I have no real lawn care or gardening advice, nor do I have any interest in trying to make anyone feel guilty about whatever practices you may or may not use on your lawn. I am certainly not wise enough to do that, nor, I hope, am I stupid enough. I am in that great middle ground

87

of ambiguity where I seem to live most of my life. What does interest me, however, is to look at the great American lawn, the well-manicured, dandelion-free lawn, as a symbol of our culture. And I'd like to try to interpret that symbol to see what it is we might learn about ourselves in the process. When I told my wife what I had in mind—this business of viewing the American lawn as a symbol of our culture—she suggested calling it "The Sermon on the Lawn," and so here we are.

Many of you have probably seen a TV commercial that I have etched in my mind. It starts out with a voice that says something like "Meet the weekend warrior—locked in a struggle with the forces of nature," and then we see this kind of Joe Average, slightly nerdy kind of guy, ready to "do battle"—with what? With his lawn, of course! And then the commercial proceeds to make a pitch for all the equipment he needs for the battle: his lawn-mower, his hedge trimmers, his edger, his spreader, his string trimmer, his watering system, and I don't know what else. It's a good-natured, light-hearted ad, but the metaphor it employs is not an accident. The motif of the American citizen, usually the American male, doing battle with the land runs very deep in our collective psyche.

The Puritans, who came over on the first boats to the New World, thought of the wilderness as the abode of the devil, a place that needed to be subdued and tamed. You can read this kind of language in the works of early American writers. And so the Puritans set out with great earnestness to conquer the wilderness. And we, as their heirs, have succeeded in this task far beyond their wildest dreams, and most likely far beyond what is healthy, either for us or for the other creatures that we share our ecosystems with. It must run very deep in the American psyche, this desire to conquer and subdue the land; to make the land conform to our standards, not the standard of the wilderness; to make the land God's land, not the devil's.

I suggest that the well-manicured lawn must, on some level, speak to us of security, of safety, of peacefulness. It must in some largely hidden, unconscious way reassure us that we and our children can sleep safely through the night without fear of attack by wild beasts or savage humans. So this is the first thing I would propose the American lawn says to us symbolically. It speaks to our deep cultural sense of wildness as dangerous

> *"I suggest that the well-manicured lawn must, on some level, speak to us of security . . . It must . . . reassure us that we and our children can sleep safely through the night without fear of attack by wild beasts or savage humans."*

and our desire to be free of that sense of danger and the fear that goes with it.

What else does the symbol say? I think it says quite a bit more. I think it says something *"One of the most important requirements of the stereotypical well-kept lawn is the absence of biodiversity."* about our cultural attitude toward biodiversity—namely, that biodiversity is not particularly valued by our culture. To a great extent, it is considered to be negative. One of the most important requirements of the stereotypical well-kept lawn is the absence of biodiversity. We call the unwanted life forms "weeds." And we use an amazing array of techniques to kill off the life forms that don't fit into our aesthetic of monoculturalism. We have a particular vehemence for dandelions, those yellow-bellied, disgusting creatures. Of course, nature itself makes no such distinctions; Mother Nature doesn't divide her children into flowers and weeds, nor do human children, by the way. What human mother hasn't been proudly presented at some point in her life with a bouquet of dandelions from a small, nondiscriminating, dirty, but loving hand? Children don't know that dandelions are weeds. They have to be taught that particular socially constructed "reality."

Of course, the dandelions will take over your yard if you let them, thereby immediately lowering the property value. I don't know about you, but I simply cannot avoid hearing the similarity between these kinds of remarks and the stereotypical remarks made when the first African-Americans move into a neighborhood. "Once they get in, they'll just take over." We tend to value monoculturalism with humans, too. And of course, it is also worth noting that the only reason the dandelions can take over the yard is because the yard is an artificially constructed, unecological monoculture to begin with. If the yard were biodiverse, the dandelions wouldn't be able to take over—an interesting lesson in ecological and perhaps even social stability.

When we do cultivate biodiversity, we don't want it to be all jumbled up together, either. We want the species to be independent, not interdependent. We want all of species A over here and all of species B over there, in clearly delineated spaces—well-defined, abstract geometric spaces, to be exact—not all mixed up together, living interdependently, "living in sin." We like clear boundaries between creatures. Perhaps that's also reassuring to us on some deep psychological level. We value independence over interdependence.

And so now we begin to see an aesthetic emerge—an aesthetic that views wildness as dangerous, perhaps even evil in some sense. An aesthetic that values monoculture over biodiversity, that divides Nature's creatures into good and evil, that labels some creatures as very evil indeed and sets out to kill them with a vengeance. An aesthetic that views interdependence as suspect, as chaos and confusion; an aesthetic that values independence, separateness, and clear, geometric boundaries as more beautiful and perhaps more reassuring psychologically. We even trim the bushes to look like geometric shapes rather than what they are.

And I would suggest to you that these qualities must be very important to us indeed, so important that we feel we must each independently (not collectively, mind you, but independently) acquire the mower (preferably a $2,000 riding mower), the edger, the trimmer, the weed whackers and spreaders and the water delivery system, to be our own weekend warrior. And in addition to all we have to acquire, we must also feel this goal in life is important enough to use precious fossil fuels to propel the highly polluting machinery and to use liberal doses of fresh water, another of our resources that is in short supply. And we must feel it important enough to supplement all of these resources with high doses of toxic chemicals designed to kill off the undesirable life forms and hopefully, through our unflinching vigilance, maintain the monocultural, unstable ecosystem that we culturally value so highly.

On top of all this, we must think it important enough to spend very significant amounts of our leisure time pursuing this goal—amazing amounts of our precious leisure time. It's really quite a cultural phenomenon, if you ask me. It must be very important to us. It must say a lot about who we are at this point in our development as human beings.

"Christianity and . . . science . . . agreed on two points: namely, that nature is not sacred, not holy . . . and they agreed that the rightful role of humans is to be the masters of nature."

Where, you might ask, does this cultural phenomenon come from? I've already suggested that it's deep within the American psyche to subdue the land, to conquer the wilderness, and I believe our lawn care culture directly reflects that heritage. But where did that philosophy of life come from? Until very recently in human history, nature was regarded as spiritual, as divine, as the source of life, beauty, and inspiration. When did that change and how did it change?

Strangely enough, this radical change came about through the unwitting cooperation of two enormous cultural forces—two forces that are usually seen as at least mildly antagonistic, but which in this case contributed to the same goal. One is Christianity and the other is science. Whatever else these two great cultural forces may have disagreed about, they both agreed on two points: namely, that nature is not sacred, not holy, not inhabited by spirit, and they agreed that the rightful role of humans is to be the masters of nature. Both Christianity and science have taught these doctrines, and both have been openly hostile toward contrary opinions.

Once Christianity became the established religion in the Roman empire, Christians systematically set about to lay waste to the sacred groves of the pagan cults. They did not want people to believe that nature was sacred. They wanted all eyes to look to their God and his son as the only sources of spiritual power. Later, Enlightenment scientists would claim that nature is totally inanimate, a bunch of billiard balls bouncing around waiting to be conquered, manipulated, and controlled by us.

The combination of these two great cultural forces was too much. Nature was unseated as being sacred, as being spiritual, as being alive, as having value in its own right, apart from its utility for human purposes. Now we're in a fix, because this way of looking at things is no longer working. And it isn't likely to get better anytime soon. We're in trouble in our relationship with Mother Nature. To paraphrase Annie Dillard, it's hard to desecrate a sacred grove and then change your mind—we have doused the burning bush and cannot rekindle it. What an amazing image!

I'm not totally sure what to do about my lawn, how to balance all the competing voices in my mind, nor do I have any interest in judging others. All of our lives are filled with contradictions and inconsistencies. But one thing I really do believe to be true is that one of the major religious issues of the next century will be the rethinking and reestablishment of some sort of

"One thing I really do believe . . . is that one of the major religious issues of the next century will be the . . . reestablishment of some sort of healthy relationship between humans and the rest of nature."

healthy relationship between humans and the rest of nature. I don't know the details of how that will work out or even whether it will work out.

There are folks who say, based on population data, that the fight is already lost, that human beings are already irreversibly doomed to intense suffering due to overpopulation and ecological deterioration. These folks remind me of an amazing story concerning the engineer who designed the Titanic. Apparently he was on board the night when the great ship hit the iceberg, and after quickly surveying the extent of the damage, he announced to the officers that the ship was doomed, even though most of the ship appeared to be undamaged. He had done the math and he knew what would happen. Some of our population biologists have done their math as well, and they are not optimistic about our future.

I don't believe that all is lost, nor do I believe that human beings are a blight on a pristine earth. That would be to fall into the same trap as the haters of dandelions. It just makes the human beings into the dandelions, the evil creatures. To use theistic language, I believe we are all God's creatures. We human beings are part of the great creative process of evolution; we are one of Nature's more interesting experiments. And an important element of the experiment is that we collectively have tremendous power to affect our own outcome.

But to make the outcome wonderful and beautiful and healthy, we will, I believe, have to give up the domination and control model of the human/nature relationship. It will have to go because it simply is not true. We are not the masters of nature. We are simply some of her creatures—powerful creatures, maybe somewhat analogous to the dinosaurs in their time, but we are not the bosses. We are going to have to change, to adapt to the truth, to grow into a new sense of identity—an identity of being fellow creatures rather than masters, an identity of humility rather than arrogance, an identity of community rather than separateness. We are going to have to find a way to reconsecrate the sacred groves, to somehow consecrate even our own little patches of earth, our own lawns. How we will do that remains to be seen, but it will be important work; it will be demanding of all of our talents, and it will be a journey of discovery about who we really are and how we can continue to flourish on this unique and precious planet.

In our Unitarian Universalist denomination, the stance of religious humanism was, up until recently at least, the predominant world view. In the last decade or so, that predominance has been questioned rather strenuously, creating a certain tension in our churches. Here is my contribution to that discussion. —MB

The Challenges for Humanism

February 2, 2002

In the early 1800s, a critical rift occurred in the Congregational churches of old New England. One of the main reasons for the split with the Congregationalists was that this new liberal group wanted to use human reason to interpret the scriptures. The more conservative of the two factions, dominated by Calvinist theology, felt that the use of reason to interpret the Bible would lead to a total breakdown of Biblical authority, and they were probably right. Nevertheless, the liberals—or Unitarians, as they came to be called—did indeed split off, and that's how the Unitarian tradition in America got started.

Well, the first thing that happened within the fledging American Unitarian Association was another split. This time the radicals who had founded the new denomination found themselves in the conservative position. The new radicals, who came to be known as the Transcendentalists—folks like Ralph Waldo Emerson and Margaret

Fuller—claimed that one didn't necessarily need the Christian scriptures for religious inspiration. One could find the truth in other scriptures, or one could learn the truth directly from nature without benefit of any scripture at all. There was quite a tussle for a while to see if the new association would be strong enough to hold both factions together. The Transcendentalists didn't last long in chronological time, but made a huge impact upon the new Unitarian movement and upon American culture in general. And the new association *did* hold together.

After the Civil War, a new group arose to challenge the liberal Christian interpretation of Unitarianism. Led by a group called the Free Religious Association, these folks wanted more emphasis on science and rational thought and less emphasis on traditional Christianity, even the liberal Unitarian kind. Again there was significant tension within Unitarianism, but the movement held together.

In the 1920s and 30s, there again arose controversy within Unitarianism; this time it was known as the humanist-theist debate. In 1933 a group of secular philosophers, Unitarian ministers, and others signed a document called the Humanist Manifesto. One of the signers was a Universalist minister named Clinton Lee Scott, who was at that time minister of this very church, which had about

1,000 members. That certainly places our church in the midst of a significant event in American religious history. The Humanist Manifesto is a fairly complex statement, but one of the things that it said quite clearly was that the time was past for virtually all forms of theism. Theism was portrayed as a kind of immature thinking that humanity had finally outgrown. The conventional wisdom within Unitarianism is that for the most part, the era of the humanist-theist debate ended with the humanists winning. Not that all Unitarian churches or all Unitarian church members went that way by any means; but the majority of Unitarians did consider themselves to be religious humanists in the 50s, 60s, and 70s, and that may be true even today.

Religious humanism is not an easy thing to define, but in general it usually is thought to include ideas such as an emphasis on civil and religious freedoms, a belief that science and reason provide the most reliable sources of human knowledge, and a rather thoroughgoing skepticism about almost all forms of theism and about religious myth and ritual in general. Religious humanism has traditionally held that *this* is the world that matters, not any other world, and that the focus of religious people should be on meeting human needs and addressing human concerns. It is a very attractive philosophy in many ways.

This little thumbnail sketch of one aspect of Unitarian history might be useful by way of providing some insight into our present situation in Unitarian Universalism, for most observers of the Unitarian Universalist scene will say that we are currently in the midst of another era of religious debate—although these things are usually easier to identify after the fact than while they are actually happening. This new era of discussion has probably been going on for the last ten or twenty years, and might be characterized as a kind of challenge to the majority position of religious humanism within our movement. Now why would such a challenge come about? That seems to me a worthwhile question to pursue for a moment.

"This new era of discussion has probably been going on for the last ten or twenty years, and might be characterized as a kind of challenge to the majority position of religious humanism within our movement."

I want to use an idea from the great scholar of religion, Huston Smith, to get started on this little exploration. Smith says that any great world view has three distinct aspects. The first he calls its "science," or we might call it its view of the facts. What is reality like? How did it come to be? The second aspect of any major world view is its teaching on social reality. How should society be organized? What should its rules and authority be? Who should be in charge? How should power flow? The third he calls its "big picture." What is life all about? What is its meaning? How do we as individuals fit into it all?

These are the three aspects of any well-developed world view that Huston Smith thinks we should examine—its view of science, or life's factual side; its view of social realities; and its view of the big picture. When we look at religious humanism in comparison to more traditional religious paths, using these three lenses, some very interesting comparisons open up to our view.

Let's try the first lens, the lens of science. Traditional religion speaks to us of a creator-god or gods and gives us mythological explanations of the origins of life that in their factual value have been clearly superceded by the creation story of modern science. Religious humanism says go with science. That's hard to argue with. Those who do argue are what we call *fundamentalists*. Religious humanism seems to have a far better answer.

Let's try the "social" lens. Traditional religions often seem outdated in their views of social reality. In many religious traditions, the fact that a certain kind of social order existed at the birth of some great teacher seems to mean that the same social order ought to exist today. So if women were discriminated against at that earlier time, it seems to justify the same discrimination today. Or if slavery was common in the ancient times, it may seem to make slavery justified in the present. This was a view taken very seriously in the era of American history prior to the Civil War.

Even today, these kinds of issues are alive and causing great pain in our world. A pronouncement about homosexuality from ancient times becomes the basis for discrimination in the present. Some ancient custom regarding whether women can fully participate in religious life becomes the argument for excluding women in the present. Religious humanism rejects all of these kinds of arguments and lifts up the modern ideals of democracy, civil liberties, and the worth and dignity of every person without regard to any outmoded caste system, class system, or other form of discrimination. Once again, religious humanism seems to be a more positive, healthy way of looking at things.

Now let's look through the third lens, the lens of "meaning," the lens with which we examine the big picture. Here's where things become less clear, in my view. One of the things that Huston Smith says about the traditional view versus the modern scientific view is that the traditional view is far more optimistic about who we are, our place in the universe, and our future. The scientific view is essentially that we are insignificant creatures without purpose who have come into being strictly by accident in a remote and infinitesimal little backwater of a vast, indifferent, unfeeling, uncaring universe. Have a nice day! According to this view, life has no meaning in and of itself, although we are free to invent one if we want to—which religious humanism, by the way, encourages us to do.

But even if we choose to invent a meaning for life, we need to face the fact that this meaning extends no further than our human imagination. Bertrand Russell, who once lectured in this church, wrote that it is ridiculous even to raise the question of the meaning of life. The very idea makes no sense. It's simply not a scientific question. By contrast, the traditional religions all say that we are important in some cosmic way, that we are glorious creatures made in the image of gods and goddesses, and that we are headed for some bright future, like heaven or enlightenment or nirvana.

". . . the traditional religions all say that we are important in some cosmic way, that we are glorious creatures . . . headed for some bright future, like heaven . . ."

Which one would you pick?

According to Smith, what we as modern folks have done is to throw out the "meaning" dimension of more traditional religious views, because those traditions had their facts wrong and their social structure was less humanistic than ours is. What he suggests is that we can continue to go back to these older traditions and mine them for their meaning and value, while at the same time acknowledging that these ancient systems have been superceded by modern science regarding the facts of life and by modern social theory regarding human rights and democratic government. And I would suggest to you that it is the effort to do precisely what Smith suggests that we have seen occurring within Unitarian Universalism in the last ten to twenty years. Some folks—certainly not all, but a significant number—have found the "meaning" dimension of religious humanism lacking, have found it unfulfilling, and have gone looking elsewhere.

In the late 1800s, Sigmund Freud looked at human behavior in a new way and made one of the most fascinating connections of all time between two very different ideas. He looked at a certain pattern of human behavior and named that pattern after an ancient myth, the myth of Oedipus. Carl Jung came along and said: you know, you can make that same kind of connection with virtually any of the ancient myths—in fact, that's how they got to be enduring stories in the first place, because they revealed some aspect of the human condition with remarkable clarity. So began the Freud/Jung/Joseph Campbell lineage with its fascination with mythology, not as a source of fact about physical reality, but as a source of understanding about who we are and what it all means. Out of that movement grew a new interest in religious ritual, which is simply the acting out of a myth. Out of that same strain grew an interest in reinterpreting ancient texts, in looking back at traditional systems of thought to reexamine them for their meanings, their values, their insights about the human condition, not for their theory of science or social theory.

This, in greatly oversimplified format, is my view on how we got to where we are now. There will be no going back to a prescientific view of the world. There will be no going back to predemocratic modes of social organization—at least I certainly hope not, and I would resist any such move with all my energy. But there is an urgent need for more of a sense of meaning in life. We are a meaning-poor culture, and I believe enormous resources do exist for us in what we might call the great wisdom traditions of humanity.

What would it mean to mine those resources while at the same time taking seriously the very real advances in human knowledge? What would such a synthesis look like? Well, I think it would look like Martin Luther King, for example. Here was someone absolutely committed to the modern humanistic ideals of freedom, civil rights, and the worth and dignity of every person. But King stirred our souls, not because he was good at talking abstract philosophy, but because he harnessed that philosophy to powerful old myths that have the capacity to motivate the human spirit—myths and stories that give meaning and establish values. "Let my people go" is not a philosophical principle, but a cry from an ancient story that, somehow or other, still has enormous power. King shows us what the synthesis can do, what it's capable of.

Perhaps faith and reason, like many other apparently contradictory principles, can coexist after all. Perhaps there is a kind of wisdom that is broad enough and deep enough to see the value of both sides of the polarity. Perhaps there is a way to be thoroughly contemporary in our acknowledgement of scientifically discovered facts and hard-won freedoms, while simultaneously finding meaning in millennia of powerful stories that say with one voice that we are connected in a meaningful way to the great cosmic force that is indeed our creator, both mythically and literally. Perhaps such a synthesis is possible—and even more importantly, perhaps this synthesis points our way to a life that is less empty and less decadent and less despairing than much of what we see in our world today. To attempt such a resolution is a challenge for each of us and for our human family. ∽

Many people have told me that this sermon helped them understand their own religious journey better. It may be particularly helpful to Unitarian Universalists, who often have a hard time defining their faith. —MB

Faith Is Not Belief

December 28, 2003

Many of us have been asked at one time or another, "Just what is it that you Unitarian Universalists believe?" And I admit this is a difficult moment, even for ministers like myself. One of the problems with this query is that the question itself makes assumptions that may not be true. In a way it's one of those questions like "When did you stop beating your children?" The hidden assumption here is that knowing what a person believes is the best way to understand and ultimately judge that person's religious life, and I for one find this assumption highly questionable.

Although the Christian faith has held belief to be its most important element, belief does not play nearly so central a role in other major religions. The crucial element in Judaism is obedience to the law, not belief. In Islam, the core of religious life is the observance of the five pillars, most of which are about doing particular things, not believing particular things. And in Zen Buddhism, belief would probably be considered irrelevant at best, and at worst an actual hindrance to the kind of clear consciousness which its spiritual practices seek to develop. So belief is certainly not universally recognized as a crucial element in religion or spirituality.

It is true that questions of belief have been very important in the history of Christianity, especially since the adoption in 325 C.E. of the Nicene Creed, which specified exactly what a Christian would need to believe to remain Christian. It is also true that questions of belief were not nearly so important in the Christian church prior to 325 C.E., when the fledgling and often persecuted religion was far more diverse and tolerant of different beliefs than it is now.

Nevertheless, Christianity ultimately chose to use points of belief as the basis to include people in, as well as to exclude people from, its fold. It used belief to separate the sheep from the goats, to use a Biblical metaphor. I think it's not unfair to suggest that elevating belief to such a high status has sometimes resulted in a rather harsh approach to religion, giving rise to the concept of heresy, and in the worst cases leading to disasters like the Inquisition. That problem certainly merits further exploration, but at this moment I'd prefer to focus attention in a different direction. What I really want to talk about here is the difference between belief and faith.

The difference between faith and belief would be a worthwhile topic for any person to explore, but I suspect it may be particularly important for those of us who are Unitarian Universalists. After all, we call ourselves a creedless religion, meaning that we don't have a specific set of beliefs that everyone must agree with. That's one of the reasons we have so much difficulty with the question about what we believe. Just as an aside, my friend and colleague Tony Larsen claims that we UUs have more beliefs than any religious group, since virtually everyone in any of our churches has his or her own complex set of beliefs. Be that as it may, I think that sometimes we may jump to the conclusion that because we don't have a creed set in stone, then it's also true that we have no faith. That would be an error of grand proportions.

". . . sometimes we may jump to the conclusion that because we don't have a creed set in stone, then it's also true that we have no faith. That would be an error of grand proportions."

I want to propose, first of all, that faith and belief are not the same thing; and second, that faith is a dimension of life that is very accessible to Unitarian Universalists as well as to folks in other religious traditions or even no tradition at all. I'm not interested in arguing that belief is a bad thing, although personally I find its value limited at best. If I had to choose between faith and belief, it would certainly be an easy choice for me; in fact, I have

110

already made that choice in my life, and the winner is faith by a wide margin. I think that we as Unitarian Universalists have a strong, vibrant faith even though, as a religious movement, we have made a very conscious decision not to limit that faith within the confines of a specific set of beliefs.

This might be a good time to bring a couple of distinguished theologians off the bench to pinch hit, just so you'll know I'm not making all this up. Listen to these words from Wilfred Cantwell Smith, one of the foremost historians of religion of the twentieth century. Belief, he says, is "the holding of certain ideas." But faith is something different:

> *Faith is deeper, richer, more personal. It is engendered by a religious tradition in some cases and to some degree by its doctrines, but it is a quality of the person and not the system. It is an orientation of the personality to oneself, to one's neighbor, to the universe; a total response, a way of seeing whatever one sees and of handling whatever one handles; a capacity to live at more than a mundane level; to see, to feel, to act in terms of a transcendent dimension. . . . Faith, then, is a quality of human living.**

*from Towards a World Theology, *by Wilfred Cantwell Smith; Orbis Books, Maryknoll, NY, 1981*

So belief is primarily the adoption of certain ideas or concepts, whereas faith, in Smith's view, is about our immediate response to the joys and concerns of life, day by day. Now listen to the words of James Fowler, who has written one of the modern classics on the subject of faith, entitled *Stages of Faith*. He characterizes faith as our response to certain questions regarding our hopes and dreams, our commitments, and what we trust in life.

> *Faith is not always religious in its content or context. To ask these questions seriously of oneself or others does not necessarily mean to elicit answers about religious commitment or belief. Faith is a person's or group's way of moving into the force field of life. It is our way of finding coherence in and giving meaning to the multiple forces and relations that make up our lives. Faith is a person's way of seeing him- or herself in relation to others against a background of shared meaning and purpose.**

So from the point of view of these two thinkers, at least, faith is very different from belief, although they certainly may coexist in the same person. But faith is not primarily about adopting a set

*from Stages of Faith *by James W. Fowler, Harper & Row, San Francisco, 1981* of beliefs. Faith is about how we respond to the joys and challenges of our lives, day by day, moment by moment. It's about whom and what we love, about where we invest our time, energy, and allegiance. It's about whom or what we trust and about how we respond in the face of difficulty and tragedy.

In the words of another great twentieth-century theologian, Paul Tillich, it's about our "ultimate concern." Or as Emerson put it, "A person will worship something." The real question is, what occupies that place in our lives?

My colleague Brooks McDaniel calls faith a kind of "courageous trust." By that I think he means that a person of faith is someone who moves forward in life, moves toward meaningful goals, trusting that his or her effort is worthwhile even in the face of difficulties, sometimes even in the face of serious doubts. These goals or ideals do not have to be concerned with getting to heaven or with any kind of other world, or even with any organized religion. They may be more related to family or community or perhaps to developing a creative

"Faith is taking the stance that somehow life is good, or at least good enough to be worth the struggle and the pain. Faith does not require that we be able to state precisely and unambiguously why that is."

113

skill. They may be focused on the pursuit of justice or providing service to others, or they might be related to a love relationship. They may even be related to a religion, although that relationship is not required for it to be faith.

Faith is a kind of stance that we take in relation to the totality of life: crazy, beautiful, comic, tragic, painful, rewarding, puzzling, inspiring life. To be a person of faith is to affirm that within this amazing kaleidoscope of life experience there is meaning available, meaning discovered or created, personal or universal. Faith is taking the stance that somehow life is good, or at least good enough to be worth the struggle and the pain. Faith does not require that we be able to state precisely and unambiguously why that is. There is no law that says we have to be able to do that. Faith can be open ended; there's nothing wrong with that approach at all. Remember the admonishment of the Tao Te Ching: "The Tao that can be named is not the true Tao."

Carl Sandburg expresses this indefiniteness of faith so well in his words, "I'm an idealist. I don't know where I'm going, but I'm on my way." What a great statement of the sense of idealism that is not tied down to a particular set of beliefs. Faith is a continuously unfolding creative process, whereas belief is all too often the tragic mistake of trying to contain that creative process inside narrow boundaries and not let it change and grow. Of course, that limitation is death to creativity, and in the worst-case scenario leads to oppression.

I'm not saying that religious beliefs can't work well in a life of faith. Clearly they can. But the beliefs need to be of the type affirmed by the great religious educator, Sophia Lyon Fahs: "gateways opening wide vistas for exploration," not "like blinders, shutting off the power to choose one's own direction." Beliefs need to be flexible and open to question, or they can too easily become oppressive.

"Faith is not about choosing something to believe in and then hanging on for dear life. . . It doesn't need to be written down, and its secret cannot be memorized and recited on demand."

Faith is not about choosing something to believe in and then hanging on for dear life. Faith lets go. Faith is trusting in the creative process of life. It is moment by moment, unpredictable, creative, open ended, spontaneous, responsive and responsible, yet always directed toward more joy, more beauty, more love, more compassion, more justice. It doesn't need to be written down, and its secret cannot be memorized and recited on demand. Listen to the message of this poem by Denise Levertov:

115

The Secret

Two girls discover
the secret of life
in a sudden line of
poetry.

I who don't know the
secret wrote
the line. They
told me

(through a third person)
they had found it
but not what it was
not even

what line it was. No doubt
by now, more than a week
later, they have forgotten
the secret,

the line, the name of
the poem. I love them
for finding what
I can't find,

and for loving me
for the line I wrote,
and for forgetting it
so that

a thousand times, till death
finds them, they may
discover it again, in other
lines

in other
happenings. And for
wanting to know it,
for

assuming there is
such a secret, yes,
for that
most of all.

—Denise Levertov

There it is, my friends, spoken by a true master. The truth is not in the words, not in any formula, but in the experience, in the heart, in the moment-by-moment response to being alive.

So if someone ever asks you, "What do you Unitarian Universalists believe?" you might say, "Ours is an open-ended, living faith," and then trust the creative process of life to let the dialogue grow and unfold as it will. ∞

Every year I participate in our city's Martin Luther King celebrations, and each year I try to say something on Sunday that will lift up his message and do justice to his memory. Here's one such attempt. —MB

The Way of Nonviolence

January 15, 1995

Martin Luther King has passed over into legend. He is no longer a flesh-and-blood human being, but a myth, a symbol, a saint. It is not necessarily a bad thing that this transformation has happened; far from it. He has become a myth where a myth was urgently needed to explain the cruel tragedy of racism in our culture and to give us hope. If he has become a twentieth-century Moses, it is certainly because we Americans deeply need a leader who can lead us all out of slavery and into the promised land. If Martin Luther King is now more legend than human being, it is quite simply because we have a deep hunger for such a legend. We are all fortunate that he came along to fill that need.

I am an unabashed supporter of the Martin Luther King holiday. There is not another national observance that focuses our attention on the ongoing tragedy of racism in our society and at the same time offers us hope that a new day can be realized by us all. We all need a hero who can proclaim that message for us, and Martin Luther King, more than any other person, was able to do that. I always find myself deeply moved by this legend of the twentieth-century Moses, and I continue to find inspiration in the story of this great modern-day prophet.

Yet I also perceive that in the process of transforming Martin Luther King from a human being into a legend, something has been lost, or is at least in danger of being lost. For me, what is in jeopardy is the human side of Martin Luther King—the sense of him as a person like you and me, and an appreciation for the deep personal and religious struggles that he went through on his unique path. Because, like all great people, Martin Luther King did not know that he was Martin Luther King. That is, he didn't know that he was going to become a symbol, a legend, a saint.

In retrospect we may tell the story of his life in that kind of storybook way where everything makes sense and all the pieces seem to fit together perfectly; but that's not the way he would have told it, I can assure you. I'll bet that he saw his own life as full of doubts, failures, accidents, twists of fate, struggles, and ambiguities, as well as triumph and success. He didn't get to be a legend by reading a book called *How to Become a Legend*. I think he was just basically a human being like the rest of us, who struggled with life issues just as we do and made a few very important commitments that thrust his rather ordinary life into a role that enabled him to make a major difference in the world. He was not larger than life, but was life itself, struggling to express itself with some kind of integrity in the face of extraordinary challenges. It's my intention here to help you find a sense of this human being, born into the family of a Baptist minister and given the weighty name of that great reformer Martin Luther.

". . . believe me, Martin Luther King was no fundamentalist. His religious reflection was sophisticated and mature. He was a religious liberal . . ."

I've been told that when the Montgomery bus boycott was being organized and the local leaders wanted to hold a meeting at King's church, he wasn't very excited about it at first. He didn't jump at the chance to become a leader. He had doubts. He was even reluctant, perhaps, to assume a leadership role.

This story, however apocryphal, is consistent with my sense of his personality. He was not an ego-dominated person at all. What, then, was the source of his strength, his will, his perseverance? In all honesty, I can only conclude that it was a genuine sense of the sacred, a genuine religious consciousness in the best sense of the word.

For believe me, Martin Luther King was no fundamentalist. His religious reflection was sophisticated and mature. He was a religious liberal; he was an educated twentieth-century man. King's religious faith was anchored in his overwhelming sense that the essence of God is love. In this, he was very much in line with our religious ancestors, the Universalists. Like the Universalists, King reasoned that if the ultimate nature of divinity is love, then that love must be capable of reconciling the deepest, the most distrustful, even the most hateful divisions between human beings. Love must be strong enough to do that, if indeed love is the ultimate power in the universe. King took deeply to heart the expression "Love thine enemies," that simplest of phrases and most difficult of all teachings to follow.

King, as a Christian in the truest and most thoughtful sense of the word, rightly perceived that this amazing, paradoxical teaching, "Love thine enemies," contained the clue to solving the most difficult challenge in his culture, the challenge of racism. It must be possible to harness this transforming power of love, to reconcile the oppressed and the oppressor, so that everyone would be liberated from an inhumane way of life.

But how could one go about doing that? What would be the technique, the method? It was in his search to answer this question that King made one of the great connections of his life: he discovered the nonviolent protest techniques of Mahatma Gandhi. This brought the issue into focus for King. It was the nonviolent, *satyagraha* philosophy of Gandhi that supplied the "how to" ingredient to go alongside the Christian teaching that love conquers all. It was the practical method of nonviolence that supplied a way for King to implement his deep religious conviction that the ultimate power in the universe is God's love. This was the foundation of King's work during his brief but highly significant lifetime. To the best of my knowledge, he never wavered from that stance. Listen to these words of Martin Luther King that were actually published after his death, having been written toward the end of his life:

> *I'm committed to nonviolence absolutely. I'm just not going to kill anybody, whether it's in Vietnam or here. I'm not going to burn down any building. . . . I plan to stand by nonviolence because I have found it to be a philosophy of life that regulates not only my dealings in the struggle for racial justice but also my dealings with people, with my own self. I will still be faithful to nonviolence.*
>
> —*Martin Luther King*

These words reflect a lifelong commitment. But today, as we try to get a somewhat realistic sense of the human Martin Luther King, let us not be lulled into thinking that King's philosophy of nonviolence was in any sense shallow or naive. He was keenly aware of the limits of the technique he was using. Listen to these words, written shortly after his return from a trip to India to study nonviolent techniques of action:

> I do not want to give the impression that nonviolence will work miracles overnight. Men are not easily moved from their mental ruts or purged of their prejudiced and irrational feelings. When the underprivileged demand freedom, the privileged first react with bitterness and resistance. . . . So the nonviolent approach does not immediately change the heart of the oppressor. It first does something to the hearts of those committed to it. It gives them new self-respect: it calls up resources of strength and courage that they did not know they had. Finally, it reaches the opponent and so stirs his conscience that reconciliation becomes a reality.
>
> —Martin Luther King

So King had no naive belief that he and his followers would just go out and practice nonviolence and everything would be okay. He knew what he was up against. One of the most moving pieces of film that I have seen is one that records the instructions King gave to a group of marchers before they went out to protest. These instructions are spiritual teachings in the deepest, most profound sense. He is saying to them, essentially, "They are going to call us names; they are going to throw things at us; they are going to do everything they can to provoke us to retaliate. But we are going to stand our ground; we are not going to let them turn us into haters. We are going to take what they dish out and stand firm and make them see the error of their ways." And then they would go out and do just that. That's faith. That's spirituality made concrete.

I have read that toward the end of his life, King became less optimistic about human nature. He went through periods of doubt and despair. But like all truly great persons, he was able to ride out his doubt and despair and somehow reconnect with the basic faith that had brought him so far along the road. In the language of depth psychology, he was able to reach deep inside and draw on the power of the archetype. He was able to connect with a sense of higher purpose when he needed to. Don't be confused into thinking he was always connected to that power. That's the legend part. The truth, I believe, is that he lost it and regained it over and over again. It's no accident that all comic book characters have both a superhero identity and a common identity, like Superman and Clark Kent. No one can be the hero all the time. We're all basically Clark Kents. But it's also true that we're all capable of connecting with a higher sense of purpose that gives us power beyond our expectations. Martin Luther King was able to do that, even in the midst of doubt and despair. Each of us has that same capability. Listen to this wonderful example of what I'm referring to:

> *After a particularly strenuous day . . .*
> *I was about to doze off when the telephone*
> *rang. An angry voice said, "Listen, nigger,*
> *we've taken all we want from you. Before*
> *next week you'll be sorry you ever came to*
> *Montgomery." I hung up, but could not*
> *sleep. It seemed that all of my fears had come*
> *down on me at once. I had reached the satu-*
> *ration point . . .*
> *"In this state of exhaustion, when*
> *my courage had almost gone, I determined*
> *to take my problem to God. . . . The words*
> *I spoke to God that night are still vivid in*
> *my memory—"I am here taking a stand for*
> *what I believe is right. But now I am afraid.*
> *The people are looking to me for leadership,*
> *and if I stand before them without strength*

and courage, they will falter. I am at the end
of my powers. I have nothing left. I've come
to the point where I can't face it alone."—At
that moment I experienced the Divine as I
had never before experienced Him. It seemed
as though I could hear the quiet assurance of
an inner voice, saying, "Stand up for righ-
teousness, stand up for truth, God will be at
your side forever." Almost at once my fears
began to pass from me. My uncertainty dis-
appeared. I was ready to face anything. The
outer situation remained the same, but God
had given me inner calm.

—Martin Luther King

Now, I know that for some of us, the idea of
a personal God who responds to prayer in this way
is not part of our experience. But I would suggest
to you that it would be equally valid to say that
what King called God is something that is inside
each of us and could just as easily be called Self or
Being or Higher Purpose. So let us not lose our
ability to hear the truth simply because it is spoken in a different theological framework than may
be our preference. Gandhi spoke the same truths
within a framework of Hinduism. We must learn
to appreciate the truth as it is spoken in many
languages. Indeed, one of the rock-bottom questions for those religious liberals who are agnostic or

atheist is how to get in touch with that same deep level of commitment that King was able to connect with. Is there a way to do that without using "god" language? We need to explore all such ways, for we will need them all.

What moves me about King's story is the picture of King as a real person, a person with the same doubts and fears we all have, and yet a person whose religious faith gave him a channel to a higher sense of purpose beyond mere ego satisfaction. What happens in this story, put in the terminology of depth psychology, is that the ego surrenders to the larger self. Then clarity results. It's a universal religious experience, whether it's described in Christian language or some other language. We all have a larger self like that. In my mind, Martin Luther King is most truly a hero because he made the decision to dedicate himself to that higher purpose. Like many others who have made such a decision, it cost him his life. But I suspect that even this was a sacrifice he was willing to make. Listen to these words of Martin

". . . one of the rock-bottom questions for those religious liberals who are agnostic or atheist is how to get in touch with that same deep level of commitment that King was able to connect with."

Luther King, a modern prophet, the last words he ever spoke in public. He was speaking in Memphis, on the eve of his assassination:

> *Well, I don't know what will happen now. We've got some difficult days ahead. But it doesn't matter with me now. Because I've been to the mountaintop. . . . And I've seen the promised land. I may not get there with you. But I want you to know tonight that we as a people will get to the promised land. And I'm happy tonight. I'm not worried about anything. I'm not fearing any man. Mine eyes have seen the glory of the coming of the Lord.*
>
> —*Martin Luther King*

That's the real thing, my friends. Human religious commitment in full bloom, human nature in full glory. There is great cause to celebrate the life of Martin Luther King. Such a man, such a full human being, has lived among us and has shown us all the way to reach the promised land. Let us celebrate that gift, and let us find the wisdom and courage to follow his lead. ∽

Lost and Found

February 4, 2002

An intriguing story is told by Harville Hendrix, well known for his books on couples therapy. He tells of a woman who came to him complaining that she had trouble thinking clearly and logically. It seems that this apparent lack of ability for logical thinking was hurting her at work, where she was being regularly passed over for promotions. It didn't take long to uncover the fact that her mother had told her repeatedly as a child that she was not very smart—not as smart as her brother, in particular. This negative message was compounded by the fact that her mother had very little confidence in her own reasoning ability as well.

When this young woman was fifteen, she had a teacher who inspired her to work harder at her schoolwork, and as a result she brought home a report card that was almost all A's. Her mother's reaction was, "How in the world did you do that? I bet you can't do that again." That particular prophecy turned out to be true, and the young woman never did well in school after that. Hendrix says she "put to sleep the part of her brain that thinks calmly and rationally."

Many of us, if not most of us, have had some experience that falls roughly into this category. Somewhere along the way of life, usually at a pretty early stage, someone told us that some part of us was broken, shameful, or just not good enough to be taken seriously; and we believed them and put that part of ourselves away somewhere in the attic part of our self. Even if we had relatively good and caring parents who didn't do anything as ill-advised as the mother in the story, we have very likely had those experiences somewhere else along the way.

When I was a kid, my father died in a car accident, and due to family circumstances I lived with relatives for about six years. These particular relatives happened to be very conservative, traditional Southern Baptists, and so of course they had a huge effect on my character formation. As I look back at that time, I'm becoming more and more aware of the good things that came out of this experience, or at least things that made me what I am. It's probably due to this early encounter with fundamentalist religion that I took the career path of becoming a Unitarian Universalist minister. How ironic.

There were quite a few messages I received during that time that fall into the same category as the mother's negative message in Harville Hendrix's story. To take one example, I was told repeatedly that dancing was morally wrong—even square dancing, if you can believe that. I can tell you that this teaching did not make my teenage years any easier, and it probably also relates directly to the fact that in the last ten years or so I have been more and more interested in learning how to dance. One of the good things that happened during that time is that I got to sing in some excellent children's choirs. Southern Baptists take their church choirs very seriously. When I left those relatives at about age twelve, I lost the opportunity to be in those choirs, and a piece of life that had given me joy just sort of disappeared. I didn't sing in a choir again until about three years ago, when I began to sing in our very own church choir right here in Peoria. These things are not mere coincidences.

". . . I was told repeatedly that dancing was morally wrong . . . and it probably . . . relates directly to the fact that in the last ten years or so I have been more and more interested in learning how to dance."

Robert Bly likes to say that when we're young, we go through life carrying a sack over our shoulder. Whenever some aspect of who we naturally are gets rejected by those around us—by our caretakers, by social convention, or maybe just because of circumstances (like my singing in the choir, or maybe it's just not cool to be that way)—that part of the self goes in the sack. It's no longer out in the open, but it's still part of who we are. Bly says that as the years go by, the sack gets heavier and heavier and weighs us down more and more. It can make life feel like a heavy burden. It can make us tired and lacking in energy and quite possibly even depressed. We have lost parts of our self; we are split and no longer whole.

Harville Hendrix calls this the lost self, and the rest of the self that's trying to make do with what's left he calls the false self. That self is not who we really are—at least not the totality of who we are by any means—but it is the self we think we have to be. So many things can get lost in this process: a skill like rational thinking or a joyful activity like dancing; it might be the sense that we're beautiful or the feeling that we're okay that gets lost. It might be that we're shamed into putting some part of our self in the sack, like some aspect of sexuality or maybe even sexuality in its entirety. Many things can go in the sack, the sack of the lost self.

One of the things that's particularly ironic about Bly's image is that here we have a picture of someone wandering through the world searching for the self, when what's sought is already present, in a sack hanging over the searcher's shoulder. What a strange coincidence! So perhaps the holy grail is very close, indeed incredibly close; it is merely hidden from view, hidden by a complicated censoring process that makes it very difficult to see indeed.

Bly says that if we spend the first half of life filling up the sack, then we spend the second half of life trying to empty the sack back out again. Piece by piece, if we choose to do so, we can recover the many amazing facets of the lost self. For each person, the specific actions needed to accomplish this will be different. It depends on what we put in the sack. For me, it seems to mean singing in the choir, learning to dance, and being a Unitarian Universalist minister, among other things. For many older men, it may mean recovering a softer, more feeling side; for some women, like the woman in our story, it may mean recovering talents and abilities that someone told us we shouldn't have. I don't know what it would mean for you, but I suspect you do know, or at least you have some hints about it—hints that could be more fully amplified given the right encouragement, like maybe a good long talk with a trusted friend. Most of us know what we need to do, or at least we know enough to get started. The rest will usually unfold once we take the first steps.

Almost all of the great religions and many of the great psychological theories tell us that the diagnosis of the human condition might be summarized as a loss of wholeness and our great longing to recover that wholeness. In the Western monotheistic traditions, one of the great images for wholeness is the Garden of Eden, where life unfolds in an uninterrupted flow of natural energy. That wonderful spontaneity is shattered, however, by an event that is not unlike the kinds of experiences that Bly and Hendrix describe. The earth creatures are told by someone pretty powerful that there is a part of experience that is forbidden; it is not okay, it is not permitted. And when they break that law, as was only natural for them to do, they are cast out of the Garden—that is, out of the experience of feeling whole, of feeling good, of feeling okay. They begin to experience shame; they begin to experience guilt; they begin to experience suffering. Somehow, as the great songwriter Joni Mitchell put it, "We've got to get ourselves back to the garden." Such is the journey of life, a journey that is probably never totally completed, but which at the very minimum gives life a sense of direction and a sense of meaning.

". . . I do believe we can reconcile self-actualization with the demands of ethics, even though I recognize there may be some significant challenges on that path."

In the Eastern traditions, that sense of wholeness is usually portrayed as having to do

134

with a certain quality of consciousness—a kind of undifferentiated consciousness, like the awakening that Buddhists refer to, or the Tao that can become a way of life. In Hinduism the term *self-realization* is used, which is highly suggestive in the context we have been exploring here. One way of visualizing the goal of our journey, then, is that it would be the realization of the fullness of the self, the realization of the totality of the self—everything out of the bag and reintegrated into a complete whole. Whitman calls it "nature without check, with original energy."

But wait, you might say. Aren't some of the things in the sack better left in there—anti-social impulses and so on? Well, the truth is that there are some things in the sack that can be problematic; that's how they got there in the first place. We can't just exercise every impulse that bursts into consciousness without any consideration for the rights and well-being of others. It's a serious matter to try to reintegrate some of the parts of the lost self. For the moment, I will just propose that there are solutions to these ethical problems. One can't say what the solution is in any particular situation without having some exploration of the particulars surrounding that situation, and this kind of exploration is probably better accomplished in private. But I do believe we can reconcile the demands of self-actualization with the demands of ethics, even though I recognize there may be some significant challenges on that path.

One thing I find uplifting and inspiring about this way of looking at things is that it says there is someplace to go in life. Life is not just a lot of aimless wandering around until we die. Life has direction. It flows in a particular way. That way is toward some kind of wholeness, some kind of completeness. That completeness may be imagined in very different ways in different traditions. There's no way around that confusing reality. What is called self-realization or self-actualization by one tradition may be called self-forgetting by another tradition and may be called an experience of God by another. This is precisely why we need interfaith dialogue. We need to learn to translate from one religious language to another.

But by whatever name, our traditions do speak with striking unanimity on this point, saying that the fullness of life is a possible experience, whether we think it comes about by meditation or therapy or prayer or exercise or dream work or good works or social transformation. The self can be whole; the experience of life can be restored from its fragmented state, at least to a great extent, at least for moments. This possibility gives life meaning and purpose, and it gives it a sense of direction. It offers us an invitation to be on our way—or perhaps The Way, if you prefer. The words will never be quite right, but nevertheless, we have an intuitive sense of where that place is, that wholeness; and when we sometimes taste its reality, we have no doubt. ∞

This sermon is just one installment in what I think of as a lifelong dialogue between science and religion. It grew out of discussions we had in one of our Thursday night classes. This is a huge topic for our period in history.—MB

In Praise of Subjectivity

January 25, 1998

A few years ago I led an adult religious education group in studying the historical Jesus. We happened, in one session, to be discussing the subject of mystical experiences—what the definition of a mystical experience was, whether people felt they had had any or not, and so on—and someone we'll call "Bill" raised a question that set me off on a particular line of thinking. Bill's very legitimate question was, as closely as I can recall it, "Aren't these experiences just due to brain chemistry?" Perhaps that doesn't sound like such a complex question, but I think that to answer it completely would probably require the construction of a full-blown metaphysical system—not a task that could be accomplished in these few pages.

What I'd like to do here instead is to try out a couple of ideas about how we might pursue this question, and also what these different approaches might imply for the field of religion. For there is no doubt that this is a very important question for all religious people, and one which fascinates and puzzles me personally as well. I don't know why I happen to like questions like that. It's probably due to my brain chemistry.

So here are a few thoughts on Bill's question, in no particular order, from one who is really only in the middle of trying to figure it out—a kind of interim report. First of all, I want to suggest that if we say a mystical experience is only due to "brain chemistry," aren't we then honor-bound to say that all human experience is only due to brain chemistry? And isn't this a true statement anyway? At least it seems so to me. All human experience is made possible by the existence and smooth functioning of the human brain and its related physiological systems. Falling in love, feeling sad, learning another language, playing a musical instrument, even doing a scientific experiment are all human experiences that, as far as we know, would be impossible without the physiological functioning of the brain. So a brain is really a pretty good thing to have around if you want to have any experiences at all; that seems pretty clear. But to say that a certain experience is due to brain chemistry probably does not distinguish it from any other experience and so really doesn't explain that experience. It doesn't tell us much about the value of that experience.

I think the difficulty arises when that little word "just" gets put in the sentence: "that's just brain chemistry" or "that's nothing but brain chemistry," as if brain chemistry were all that was needed to explain a particular phenomenon. I would suggest that this kind of "nothing-but-ery" can get us into a lot of trouble. Let's suppose for a moment that we're listening to an opera by Mozart. If we're not dead, and if we have any appreciation for this type of music, this is very likely a pretty complex and intense experience for us. Would it make sense to say that this complex experience is nothing but brain chemistry? Would that be an adequate description of the experience? Or would it be adequate to say that this experience is nothing but some sound waves hitting one's eardrums and producing audio sensations? Or would it be accurate to say that this experience is nothing but one more expression of a morally bankrupt European aristocratic culture that amused itself with the arts while keeping the masses starving? Or should we explain this experience by saying it is nothing but an example of the classical period in Western music? Aren't all of these statements true in a way, or at least can-

". . . all of these explanations have value within a certain interpretive framework. . . . To say that one of them has the only important truth . . . seems to me at best unwise and at worst tyrannical."

didates for the truth, subject to counterargument and interpretation?

Now what if someone at the opera says that listening to the opera is a deeply moving experience for her or for him? Is this experience explained away by any of the other interpretations of how the brain works? I think that it is not. In fact, I think all of these explanations have value within a certain interpretive framework. Each has a piece of the truth, like the blind people and the elephant. To say that one of them has the only important truth, and all the other truths are insignificant, seems to me at best unwise and at worst tyrannical. So one very important truth in this situation seems to be that a particular explanation or description of a phenomenon within a certain discipline does not invalidate all other descriptions of that event by other disciplines.

Now let's consider the last of these examples, the person who said this was a "deeply moving experience." This person may be in the most vulnerable position of all, because this person's experience may be said to be purely subjective. In our culture, it seems to be almost illegitimate somehow to say that something is purely subjective. This distrust, I think, goes back to what's called in Western philosophy the mind-body problem. The question is, does the mind have any value at all, or any real existence at all? Or is it really just a kind of epiphenomenon—or side effect, as it were—of other causes, like brain chemistry?

To the best of my knowledge, there are four main ways to answer this question; of course there are undoubtedly more, but at least these are four of the big ones. One very well-known one is Descartes' answer that mind and body are two different things entirely. We have a body and we have a mind, and they are definitely not the same thing. The mind inhabits the body, a kind of ghost in the machine that has its own separate existence. This is called dualism, and it's not very popular anymore. It is rather compatible with some older religious views that emphasize an immortal soul that doesn't need a body to exist; but the problem is that no one seems to be able to locate that soul, and therefore many people are skeptical that it exists, at least in this old traditional way.

"Materialism is a kind of reductionism. It reduces all phenomena to the interaction of matter; there is no mind or soul or spirit to muddy up the picture."

As science got into full swing, Descartes' view became less and less popular, and the view that replaced it for many people was the view that there is no mind, just bodies. This is called materialism. I think the view that a mystical experience is just due to brain chemistry could accurately be classified as materialist. Materialism is a kind of reductionism. It reduces all phenomena to the interaction of matter; there is no mind or soul or spirit to muddy up the picture. Materialism has enjoyed a pretty long run of popularity in our Western culture, but in the last hundred years or so it has come under some serious scrutiny, especially as a result of some of the findings of twentieth-century physics, which I will have something more to say about shortly.

A third way of solving the problem is a more contemporary one that goes by the name of functionalism. Functionalists use analogies like hardware and software to explain body and mind. The mind is not the hardware, but the software—the organizational principle behind the physical stuff. The analogy with a computer is certainly very appealing in a time when computers are everywhere in our culture. So the mind or soul or self is really not a thing at all, it's an organizing principle. It's like the Mozart opera. Where does the music exist? We may see a particular performance of the music or see the music printed in a musical score, but is that the music? Where is the music itself? Perhaps the mind is like that, say the functionalists. It's software; it's a set of ideas. We may see it or store it in a physical form, but that physical form is not the music itself. That's something different. This idea of mind is very close, I think, to what the ancient Greek philosophers called *logos*.

A fourth way to talk about this issue is one that has been more and more used and explored as a result of certain findings of twentieth-century physics. As I understand the matter, the branch of physics known as quantum mechanics—which apparently is a pretty practical enterprise that yields repeatable results—says that in measuring certain kinds of physical phenomena at subatomic levels, it becomes apparent that the existence of the observer, or perhaps we should say the act of observation, has an effect on determining the reality that is observed. The subject influences the object, and even to some extent determines the characteristics of the object observed. Now, this is not just ordinary Physics 101. This is very different. Why? Because the goal of scientific experiments in general is to reduce the impact of the observer—to zero if possible—so that the knowledge gained is objective. But quantum mechanics says that at these subatomic levels of creation, this is not possible. The subject must affect the object.

". . .in measuring certain kinds of physical phenomena at subatomic levels, it becomes apparent that the existence of the observer . . . has an effect on determining the reality that is observed."

So this view of reality says that subjectivity is not something that can ever be gotten rid of; it's part of the way things are, in some mysterious and very fundamental way. Experience is not a subject looking at an object, but really more like a subject who is also a kind of object, looking at a subject-object interaction. John Wheeler, a physicist whose wonderful drawing is shown here, says things like, "A scientist

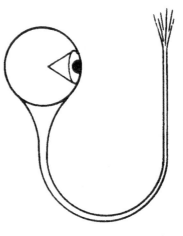

drawing by John Wheeler; from God and the New Physics *by Paul Davies: Simon and Shuster, pub.*

is an atom's way of looking at itself." Wheeler goes so far as to say that an act of observation in the present can actually have an influence on the past. I can't explain to you how this works, but I know that this scientist is considered sane by his peers, even though this theory might sound like an episode of *Star Trek*.

So this fourth view, which I think grows mainly out of a twentieth-century view of physics, asserts something quite remarkable—that subjectivity is inherent in the nature of things and cannot be separated from material existence, from so-called objective reality. Alfred North Whitehead and Charles Hartshorne, a philosopher and a theologian respectively, drew heavily on this idea in creating a theological system known as process theology. Process theology asserts that both subjectivity and objectivity are present in every event. It further states that the ultimate building blocks of reality are not made of matter, but of what Whitehead calls "actual entities," which are little bits of experience, little bits of subject-object interaction, or as William James put it, "drops of experience." This is pretty amazing stuff. According to the process theologians, then, everything in the universe is made up of bits of experience. If you think about it, this is very close to what the quantum mechanics folks are saying—namely, that subatomic events can be understood only as the interaction of subject and object, or, as Whitehead and Hartshorne would say, "occasions of experience." So that's the fourth way to answer Bill's question, to say that subjectivity is in the nature of reality itself and is in fact part of how things are.

"Process theology asserts that both subjectivity and objectivity are present in every event. . . . that the ultimate building blocks of reality are not made of matter, but of . . . little bits of experience."

And as long as I've gone this far, we might as well close the loop and say that this fourth view is highly resonant with many spiritual and religious teachings, both ancient and contemporary. There is a wonderful place in the Hebrew scriptures where Abraham asks God who He is, and God replies, "I am that I am." What an amazing answer! "I am that I am," or we might say, "I am pure subjectivity." I am the "I," the consciousness, the software of the universe. For those of you who like Sally McFague's fascinating metaphor of the physical universe as the body of God, the corresponding subjective aspect of God would be this "I am that I am," this magnificent affirmation of subjectivity.

Obviously these are only speculations and thought excursions, but they are, in fact, important. I think Western civilization right now is taking a turn in a direction away from the ideal of purely objective knowledge. That's part of what postmodernism is all about. I think our culture is becoming more and more convinced that such a thing as complete objectivity does not exist. The knower is always involved in the knowing. We are nature looking at nature, nature looking at herself. There is no place outside of nature to stand and get a better look, no observation tower outside the system. We are always inside the picture we are looking at. We are the picture looking at itself.

Does that mean we should give up reason and critical thinking? Of course not. On the contrary, we need to get better at reason and critical thinking. We need all the human faculties in the best working order possible. But neither should we give up feeling, loving, commitment, faith, or even mystical experience. The postmodern world is an exciting place, much stranger and more complex than the one that is being left behind. I find it invigorating. That's a subjective experience of mine and one that excites me, strange entity that I am, so full of hopes and dreams, so full of subjective experience and brain chemistry.

Welcome to the world of spirituality and religion, one of the greatest chemistry experiments of all time. ∞

Better Living Through Alchemy

January 4, 1998

Psalm 1
Blessed are the man and the woman
who have grown beyond their greed
and have put an end to their hatred
and no longer nourish illusions.
But they delight in the way things
    are
and keep their hearts open, day and
    night.
They are like trees planted near
    flowing rivers,
which bear fruit when they are
    ready.
Their leaves will not fall or wither.
Everything they do will succeed.

For quite some time now, I have been thinking about doing a sermon on the symbolism of the medieval art known as alchemy. You may wonder why I would want to do a thing like that; after all, I am a reasonably well-respected minister in a rather conventional Midwestern city, and alchemy—the effort to transform lead into gold—is, to put it mildly, something that just plain didn't work. So why talk about something that was such a complete failure? Especially in a congregation with so many bona fide chemists, the people who replaced alchemists historically and whose processes have worked remarkably well. Why do such a thing? I wouldn't blame you if you thought that the poor old minister had really lost his marbles this time. I, too, have had that thought.

But on the other hand, as much as it is true that the medieval alchemists were complete and utter failures at their goal of turning lead into gold, it is also true that sometimes in the midst of such colossal failures, some real discovery can be made—perhaps something the discoverer wasn't even looking for. The discovery of America by Columbus is one striking example of such an unanticipated and unintended discovery, but there are many others as well. The history of science is full of stories of discoveries that were made by accident or unexpectedly. So what looks like a failure at one point in time may look like a success later on when seen through different lenses. And so it may be with the alchemists, those strange men and women who spent long hours heating and cooling and mixing various metals in hopes of somehow, some way, creating gold—creating that which was felt to have the highest value one could imagine.

Carl Jung, a protégé of Freud who eventually broke with his teacher and founded his own brand of psychoanalysis, which would become known as analytical psychology, believed that the alchemists were on to something; but it wasn't a way to turn lead into gold—at least not literally. What Jung saw in the apparently meaningless rambling of the alchemists was that in the absence of any real scientific tools to use in their search, they had turned inward—perhaps partly intentionally, partly not—into their own minds, into their own psychological landscapes. And he saw

". . . they were an enormous distance away from what they had set out to discover; but . . . they may have been right on top of some very significant discoveries . . ."

that by the intensity of this inner psychological reflection, they had created some remarkable maps of human development—maps that, if we can decipher them, will yield up some fascinating psychological insights that may be useful to us now, hundreds of years later. Like Columbus, they were an enormous distance away from what they had set out to discover; but also like Columbus, they may have been right on top of some very significant discoveries of the highest value.

And so at great risk to my reputation, I want to walk us through a set of alchemical drawings, to see if we can catch any glimpses of new lands worth exploring—any little nuggets of gold. These drawings are from the *Rosarium Philosophorum*, a medieval alchemical text. The purpose of the drawings, from an alchemical standpoint, was to illustrate how the properties of masculine and feminine—which were believed to be present in different proportions in different metals—could be put through various kinds of chemical interactions in the process of producing gold. Of course, this line of thought went nowhere at all in the field of chemistry, but the interaction of masculine and feminine—we might say the polarity of masculine and feminine—has continued to fascinate human psyches of both genders down through the ages. What Jung suggests is that these drawings, while having no value at all in the field of chemistry, have in fact wonderful value in the field of psychology and do actually provide an accurate model of how intimate love relationships work. So let me see if I can walk us through the drawings, interpreting them psychologically as the course of development of an intimate relationship.

My disclaimer is to emphasize that I am not an expert on the subject, but I have for some time been an interested and eager student. I also want to acknowledge the great assistance of a fascinating book entitled *Coming Together—Coming Apart* by John Desteian, and also the wonderful lectures of

David Dalrymple, a Jungian analyst who lives in Rockford, Illinois, and who, interestingly enough, is also a UU minister. I appreciate their help, but I still want to say that I present this material to you as a kind of exploration. I do not present it as dogma nor as creed, nor do I present it to you as if I were a therapist. I do not offer any advice. I speak as a minister, and as an explorer who looks for ways to understand this puzzling life that we've been given, and for ways to heal the wounds that seem to be part of the package.

Picture 1

We'll begin with Picture #1, the mandala fountain. This picture gives us a model of reality—or, in this case, of psychological reality. The sun and moon symbols suggest that masculine and feminine are both present in nature, a polarity deeply imbedded in the natural order. The fountain suggests that reality is creative, that novelty is constantly being introduced from some underground source, like a well. The well, from a psychological point of view, would represent the

153

unconscious mind. The circular fountain suggests a kind of zodiac or clock or image of the seasons. So we might say that the psyche manifests through

Picture 2

time by bringing up the contents of the unconscious into consciousness, and that when that manifestation takes place, masculine and feminine are one of the pairs of opposites that appear.

It is in this broader context that our intimate relationships take place. This is the setting for our story. "Once upon a time," we might say, "there was a land called the human psyche . . ." And so our story begins.

Picture #2 begins the drama of an individual relationship. This picture illustrates the moment of meeting—the moment when two strangers' eyes meet and something magical happens. Strangely enough, we sometimes call that magical something "chemistry." What is it that happens with this particular meeting of eyes that does not happen in the dozens of other meetings we have every day of the year; what is this so-called chemistry? I need to digress here for a moment in order to explain that process—that "chemistry"—from a Jungian point of view.

According to Jung's theory, every man carries in his unconscious an image of his ideal woman, and likewise, every woman carries an image of her ideal man. Jung calls these images *anima* and *animus*, respectively. Where do they come from? Well, they come from childhood experiences, mostly, and perhaps also partly from cultural norms. Harville Hendrix calls this image the *imago*, wisely degenderizing it. I'm going to call this ideal image the dream lover or ideal lover, and that way it works equally well for different genders and also for different sexual orientations. Whatever we call it, it's our internal image of our ideal love partner.

What this "chemistry" amounts to, then, is that when we meet someone who seems to match the internal image we already have, we project onto that person the identity of our ideal dream lover. We unconsciously decide that this person is The One. And if it works for the other as well, if both parties do this, we get a double projection, and that is powerful stuff; that's the stuff of movie scenes on a starlit night. A person in the grip of this kind of projection says things like, "I feel like I've known you my whole life"—which is absolutely true, since this person has, indeed, known this lover internally for a long time, and now simply feels they're meeting in the flesh. This experience is called falling in love or, as John Desteian calls it, less poetically but perhaps more accurately, infatuation.

In Picture #3 we see a symbolic representation of the kind of totally uncharacteristic self-revelation that usually follows the initial experience of falling in love. The partners bare their souls to each other, telling their life stories, sharing hidden parts of themselves that they ordinarily keep secret, acting in ways that they usually

Picture 3

wouldn't dream of acting. We might say the reason they do these things is that the very nature of the act of projection of the unconscious dream lover is to let loose parts of the psyche that have been hidden up until now. There is a lowering of the usual defenses that keep the unconscious under control. The dream lover is out, the gate is open, and secret, hidden dimensions of the personality rush out.

Introverts sing at the karaoke bar, macho guys go to poetry readings. Life is full, animated, inspired, energetic, and unconventional. We feel a rush of energy. We are in love!

In Picture #4 we see the lovers in the bath, or perhaps it's a kind of medieval hot tub. Water often symbolizes the unconscious, so we might say the relationship is now showing both a conscious aspect and an unconscious aspect; or we might even say there is a conscious relationship between the two partners and an unconscious,

Picture 4

unseen relationship between the two dream lovers. People in this stage often say things like, "I can't live without you," which we hear constantly, by the way, in popular music. "I can't live without you" is a symbol of being in the grip of very powerful unconscious forces—forces so strong that we may feel we have no identity at all outside the relationship. "My life is empty without you, dear"—as one song says—is a pretty strong statement about how powerful these forces really are. It's also a pretty scary statement, when you stop and think about it.

157

In Picture #5 the lovers reach a culminating point in their relationship. The alchemical drawing shows it as a sexual union, but psychologically it

Picture 5

is probably more akin to a declaration of love or to a wedding. A union of lives takes place, or at least as much of a union as the partners are capable of. The unity candle is lit, the two become one, the separate lives are joined. And therefore, from now on the pictures of the partners are drawn as one hermaphroditic being. They have in fact become one, psychologically. They are so intertwined that they function almost as a single being.

Note also that the joining takes place in the water; that is to say, it is a union in which much that is going on is happening on an unconscious level. In such a state there is ecstasy, there is joy, but probably not much understanding of what is actually taking place. The lovers quite literally don't know what they're doing. There is also a kind of transcendence of the ego in this state; both of the individual egos are subordinated to the new relationship. Transcendence gives this experience

158

a spiritual quality, which seems to me to be part of the reason even nonreligious couples often want a church wedding. Intuitively or unconsciously, they rightly sense that this is a spiritual moment, a transcendent moment. If only it could last . . . but, alas, it never has.

Picture #6 shows the united couple in the tomb. A death has taken place. But why? There are several ways we might look at it. One is to remember that in the union in Picture #5, there was a subordination of the ego to the greater reality of the relationship. The ego doesn't like being transcended and has a natural tendency to reassert itself, overthrowing the wonderful "in love" feeling. Along with this development, it

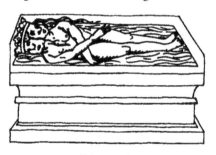

Picture 6

is also likely, if not inevitable, that the projection of each partner's dream lover or ideal lover onto the other cannot last. Each partner must at some point become painfully aware that he or she has not, in fact, married the ideal lover, but instead has married a very imperfect and at times downright irritating human being. This is an enormous disappointment to both partners, and with the illusion shattered and the egos reasserted after the all-too-

159

brief interval of transcendence, the perfect pinnacle of love is soon lost. What often takes its place is a battle of disappointed, upset egos, each trying to get the other to do what it wants. The blissful union has died.

Now at this point, several different things might happen. One is that the couple splits up and that each person, after a period of grieving, goes back to Picture #2 with a new partner and starts over. This is a very popular way to go in our culture. Sometimes people spend years in this kind of pattern, which computer programmers might call an infinite loop. Another possibility is that they stay together but cease to have any kind of intimate relationship. You can sometimes see these couples in restaurants. They don't speak; they don't even look at each other. They appear unrelated. They are united in a dead relationship.

Picture #7 shows another possibility. In this picture we see the soul leaving the body. This might mean several things. It certainly means that the soul has gone out of the relationship. But it also means that in each partner, the ideal or dream lover, which is also a kind of soul-image, breaks its projection onto the other partner and flies off somewhere else. This somewhere else may possibly be an affair, or perhaps just the temptation to have an affair, or it might be a new career or a new interest that one becomes passionate about. It might be a musical instrument or a social cause or a spiritual awakening of some kind. In any case, it is a change that demonstrates beyond any doubt that it is no longer true that "my life is empty without you, babe." In fact, exactly the opposite has become true. My life is empty with you, babe, but over here it is full. Of course, during this time it is quite likely that the couple may break up. But if they don't, if

Picture 7

they stay together, with the power of the projection broken, then something altogether different may begin to happen, which is shown symbolically in Picture #8.

In the Bible story of Gideon, Gideon asks God for proof that He/She exists and will help him. The proof that Gideon requests is for God to send the dewdrops from the sky to fall on one specific place and no other. From a Jungian point of view, God is a symbol for the self, the much deeper and more inclusive sense of identity beyond the normal ego identity. What happens in Picture #8 is that if each partner withdraws the projection of the ideal

161

lover from his or her partner, but does not transfer it to someone else right away, a period of self-examination can be entered into in which the partner becomes aware of this deeper sense of self. In the

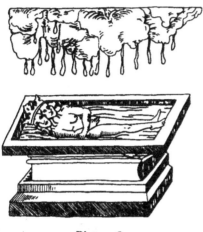

Picture 8

Gideon story, this would be the equivalent of becoming aware of the presence of God. To do this, each party must do his or her own inner work. Each partner realizes that the dream lover is an inner reality, not an outer one, and each partner also works to understand negative thoughts and upsets as his or her own, and not as something belonging to a "worthless" partner. As the spell of projection is broken and the required inner work is completed, each of the partners can begin to experience himself or herself individually as being healed, as becoming a more whole person. The dewdrops, then, represent the recovered or healed parts of the lost self. The dewdrops may be tears as well, because there could be grief during this stage. But they are healing tears; they are the tears of becoming aware

162

of the existence of a deeper, more conscious, less deluded, more adult and more responsible self.

If the partners have the courage and perseverance to go through this kind of self-work, Picture #9 says that there will be a reanimation of the relationship. The soul of the relationship will be restored. The birds in Picture #9 are puzzling. Why are those birds there? And why is one of them partially buried in the ground? I suspect that the bird is a symbol of nature, of the instinctual side of life, and that its presence shows that this instinctual, often unconscious side of life also has to be accepted and integrated into the expanded identity of each of the part-

ners. So the dream lover, the shadow of negativity, the natural instincts, and the unconscious have now been integrated into the self.

Picture 9

The lovers now finally emerge from the tomb.

They are reborn psychologically and spiritually; their marriage of lead has become a marriage of gold. They are each both male and female, both ego and shadow, both conscious and unconscious;

they are each complete as an individual; they are each finally free from having to try to find themselves in someone else. They are now able to see each other as real people, not as projections. They are free for the first time to, in fact, have a relationship of real love. The transformation is complete, as shown in Picture #10. Not only are they complete, but they are ready to bring forth fruit, either literal or metaphorical children. They enhance the quality of life in the world. "They are like trees planted near flowing rivers which bear fruit . . . everything they do will succeed."

Picture 10

I don't know how much of your own life you may see in these ancient pictures, originally drawn for a purpose very different from the way we're using them here. As always, I will leave it to you to determine the usefulness of this model for your own life. I don't mean it as a way of giving

164

cheap advice, or of telling anyone what he or she should do.

I do, however, think it is absolutely fascinating that these eccentric old alchemists would have come up with these ideas in their pursuit of a very different goal. I do find that this model makes me take seriously Jung's idea that there are basic patterns of life that are deeply ingrained in the human psyche and that manifest themselves both in cultural artifacts and in our personal lives. I do find it extremely refreshing to work with models like this one that proclaim that all of our searching and suffering and loving and leaving and returning have some sense to their pattern; that life is not just about enduring and adapting, but also about growing and getting somewhere very meaningful. I do find it worth noting, as well, that this model affirms the value of long-term committed relationships—not because they are so blissful all the time, which they aren't, but because through them we have the best chance to grow into the fullness of life. As a spiritual and religious person, I affirm, along with this

"I do find that this model makes me take seriously Jung's idea that there are basic patterns of life that are deeply ingrained in the human psyche and that manifest themselves both in cultural artifacts and in our personal lives."

view, that life does not move just randomly, but rather in a definite developmental direction; and that if we are willing to take that journey, then at some point down that road we will find, not a literal pot of gold, but something even more valuable, something truly sacred and deeply fulfilling. We will find both our own true selves and the infinitely precious ability to truly love someone. May we all complete that journey. ∞

Anyone who tries to define God is probably in trouble right away, but like so many others, I couldn't resist trying.—MB

A Definition of God

For some good reason, which I can no longer remember, at some point I decided it would be a good idea to attempt to formulate a definition of God. I do remember clearly that it made sense at the time. As I recall, I had the idea of coming up with a long, complex, half-playful and half-serious definition that would sum up my personal thoughts about the God symbol at this stage in my life. But that no longer seems like such a good idea. As a matter of fact, the famous line from the Tao Te Ching makes it very clear that all such attempts are doomed to failure: "The Tao that can be named is not the true Tao."

The same idea occurs in Judaism with the prohibition against making any image of God. All such images are at best mistaken and at worst misleading. So all the words are wrong, and all the pictures are wrong as well. Not a very promising start, is it? And yet we human beings as a whole are fascinated with various ideas of God, even those of us who say we don't believe in any such idea. Listen to the words of Diana Eck, a professor at Harvard

Divinity School and a leading scholar in the field of world religions:

> *All of us, in almost every religious tradition, live our lives with a theology of sorts, whether we think about God as father or mother, lover or hero, tyrant or thousand-armed protector. Even if we think more abstractly of the "ground of being," "depth dimension," or "ultimate concern," as Tillich would put it, or think of God as absent, meaningless, a foolish idea and an outworn name, we still have a theology in the sense that we have made some evaluative decisions about the meaning of the term God for ourselves. Even those who are uncomfortable with the term God or who reject God, have an idea and an image of God.*
>
> *—Diana Eck*

This last part is particularly interesting to me—the idea that even those who reject the notion of God have an idea of God, an idea of what God is supposed to be. Another writer has said that atheism is always the rejection of some *particular idea* of God. According to this theory, first we have an idea of God, and then we reject it. Whether that's always true or not I will leave to you to decide, but it's a fascinating notion. I myself, when asked by someone whether I believe in God, usually ask the questioner to tell me what he or she means by that word "God." It could make a lot of difference in my answer. It could be the difference between yes and no.

So what we mean by "God" might turn out to be rather important. Whatever we might mean by the word, the fact is that in one form or another, one idea or another, god or goddess, Christian or Hindu, the idea of God is extraordinarily widespread and incredibly influential in the human culture on this planet. It is an extraordinarily deeply-rooted human notion about the way things are. As Carl Jung once said when asked if he thought there really was a God, "God is a psychological reality!"

So maybe that is the place to begin, with the psychological reality. Maybe the place to begin is with human experience. What is there in human experience that makes this idea of God or Goddess occur over and over again in human consciousness, in different cultures, at different times and in different ways, but with an impressive degree of universality? Why does that happen? I want to offer a possible explanation, and I will leave it to you to decide whether that rings true with you or not, as we always do in our liberal religious tradition.

It seems to me that we, as human beings, have a nearly universal intuition that we exist in a world not of our own making and fairly often not even to our liking. We did not choose this world or this life. It was simply given to us, given to us by someone or something that is responsible for the conditions of living and the very fact of our existence. So far I think we're dealing with more or less universal perceptions. This "givenness" of the conditions of life and the sense of some source outside ourselves that's responsible for these conditions are, I think, pretty widely agreed on. Now I'm not yet saying anything about what this mysterious thing is like—I'm just saying that something totally out of our control happened, and here we are!

The real question is, of course, what is this source like? Is it conscious or unconscious, personal or impersonal, caring or indifferent? Is it male or female or neither or both; is it purely material, or does it have a subjective dimension; can it hear me if I talk to it, or is it totally deaf? Does it care at all what happens to me or you or any of the incredible multitude of creatures it has apparently created? Does it love us? These are pretty tough questions. And depending upon how one answers them, one may be classified with a label like theist or atheist or agnostic or whatever.

If one seems to be a member of the theist club, or in that general ballpark, one's answers to these questions would also suggest what kind of god or goddess one might believe in: the angry Yahweh; the self-sacrificing Jesus; the both loving and angry goddess Kali; the playful Krishna; the bountiful nurturer Mother Divine; the abstract scientific god of Einstein; the ever-changing, creative, adventurous god of the process theologians; or the mystical god of Meister Eckhart. And these are, of course, only a very small number of the possibilities.

If one is inclined more toward the types of answers that we humans seem to lump together under the atheist and agnostic labels, the answers to the questions still provide for a wide range of positions. Is it nature we see as the source of the "givenness" of life, and if so, what is this nature like? Is it evolutionary or directionless; is it benevolent or indifferent; is it orderly or random; is it knowable or unfathomable; is it moral or amoral; is it intrinsically creative or merely accidental; is it completely explainable in materialistic terms, or does it require a dimension of consciousness to be understood? Is it completely explainable at all? So the questions and the possibilities are quite numerous and really far beyond the rather too simplistic dichotomy of atheist and theist—even beyond the trinitarian version of athe-

". . . the questions and the possibilities are quite numerous and really far beyond the rather too simplistic dichotomy of atheist and theist. . . Thank goodness theology and religion are far richer than that."

ist, theist, and agnostic. Thank goodness theology and religion are far richer than that.

I am certainly not going to try to answer all of these questions here, nor would I be up to the task. There is a lifetime supply of such questions and then some. However, I would like to suggest pretty strongly that the atheist/theist distinction is vastly overemphasized in our world. It really tells us very little and leaves the most important questions unanswered. My personal observation is that everyone acknowledges that we live and move and have our being as creatures swimming in a vast matrix of reality that is enormously more powerful than we are and of which we are, in fact, a part.

The essential question of religion is not what name we should give to this mysterious something. A far more important question is this: what kind of relationship do we want to have with that larger reality which is our source, our home, and our destination? Should we worship it, try to conquer it, love it, listen to it, talk to it, manipulate it, study it, praise it, merge with it, or attempt to explain it? What do we do with this larger reality—a reality that is not only where we live but, in a very real sense, who we are? What I'm trying to suggest is that the question of what stance we take relative to this larger reality is far more important than the name we give it, be it God or Nature or Goddess or the Transcendent or the Void or Emptiness or the

Universe. All of these names are wrong anyway. We established that right from the start.

What stance do we take relative to that reality? Now that is a meaningful question. Almost all religious traditions, and quite a few secular philosophical traditions as well, give similar answers to this question—amazingly similar, in fact. The main answer that so many traditions give is that the health of the individual consists in being intimately related to this larger reality, in honoring it, and in some sense serving it, in some sense subordinating one's self to it. Here is how Emerson says it:

> I am constrained every moment to acknowledge a higher origin for events than the will I call mine. . . . There is deep power in which we exist and whose beatitude is accessible to us. Every moment when the individual feels invaded by it is memorable. . . . The soul's health consists in the fullness of its reception. . . . Within us is the soul of the whole; the wise silence, the universal beauty, to which every part and particle is equally related; the eternal One. When it breaks through our intellect, it is genius; when it breathes through our will, it is virtue; when it flows through our affections, it is love.
>
> —Ralph Waldo Emerson

Such is Emerson's view. Emerson believes, and I am with him on this one, that the positive, meaningful aspects of life emerge from this receptivity or contact with the larger reality—what he calls the "Over-soul." These meaningful dimensions of life are things like beauty, truth, goodness, and love. In more traditional language we might say, "Every good gift and every perfect gift comes from above." Most of us are no longer receptive to that kind of language—it strikes us as perhaps antiquated and quaint—but the sense is very much the same. We just have to translate from one kind of religious language to another.

If Emerson is right about this, and I believe he is, then one of the most important things for us to do in life is to participate in activities that put us in touch with the larger reality—the Over-soul, or what Charles Hartshorne calls "the wholeness of the world," which is about as close as I can get to a definition of God. The "wholeness of the world" calls to us to respond to it with our whole being. As a matter of fact, Hartshorne, a process theologian, defines worship as paying attention with the fullness of our being: mind, body, intellect, spirit, and emotions. It is paying attention with the wholeness of the self. So worship is one way to respond to the wholeness of the world with our whole being. I'm sure we can all think of other ways—perhaps things like nature hikes, meditation, working for justice in human society, prayer, tai chi, or contemplating the stars.

I'm convinced that scientific investigation is another such technique, at least when practiced in a certain frame of mind. It's a way of communing with the great source of order in the universe and conversing with it. An experiment is a question. The results are the answer. The answer may be cryptic or even confusing, but isn't that true of all conversation? Our job as religious people is not so much to figure out the right name for this wholeness of the world as it is to open our hearts to it and to respond to its needs as they unfold to us. We see those needs always only in part—in the eyes of a hungry child, in the plight of a rain forest whose billions of inhabitants are threatened, in the hole in the ozone layer around our delicate planet. If we are sensitive, we can see these needs in every experience we have.

". . . worship is one way to respond to the wholeness of the world with our whole being. I'm sure we can all think of other ways—perhaps things like nature hikes, meditation, working for justice in human society, prayer, tai chi, or contemplating the stars."

At the same time, we are called to be receptive to the beauty of this wholeness, to appreciate it and delight in its fullness. Contact with nature and wildness is one way to do that; another, more inward, way is meditation in its many forms. Meditation is nothing more or less than systematically opening our minds and hearts to the wholeness of the world. When one becomes truly aware of this wholeness, through meditation or walking in the woods or by any other way, we call this a mystical experience, and it is described in remarkably similar terms by people who have had such experiences, whatever their cultural background. Emerson clearly had such experiences on a regular basis. Einstein seems to mean something very similar to this when he describes what he calls "the cosmic religious sense." Such experiences are not about belief or dogma or creed or worn-out myths; they are about becoming aware of the wholeness of the world, by whatever name we may call it.

"When one becomes truly aware of this wholeness, through meditation or walking in the woods or by any other way, we call this a mystical experience, and it is described in remarkably similar terms by people who have had such experiences, whatever their cultural background."

Bring many names: they are all imperfect. But the thing itself is still real, the experiences people have are very real, and the sense of liberation and of being lifted up that comes from such experiences is totally real. Religious language may go out of date, but the wholeness of the world is not out of style or worn out. Our job is to appreciate that wholeness, to feel its beauty and magnificence, to not take our names for it too seriously, and to develop our own sense of individual wholeness through an intimate relationship with that cosmic wholeness which has no name, but which is, in fact, our home, our journey, and who we really are. ∽

What can one say on Christmas Eve that hasn't already been said? Every year, if we are fortunate, we may discover the meaning of the holiday all over again.—MB

Follow Your Star

December 24, 1997

It really is amazing how long the Christmas story has lasted and how popular it still is. It's certainly one of the best known stories in the whole world. When a story is that well known and has lasted that long, you can be sure it must tell us something pretty valuable about this life of ours and about who we are.

The best stories usually have many meanings, not just one. With a really good story, you can hear it over and over again and keep hearing new things each time. The Christmas story has lots of interesting characters: the baby Jesus, Joseph and Mary, the shepherds, the kings, the innkeeper, the angels, the star—each of them is like a different part of who we are; each of them tells us something about ourselves. Any one of them would be worth thinking about.

This Christmas season, I have felt particularly intrigued by the star. What is that star doing there anyway? Some astronomers have tried to look back in history to see if there might have been some astronomical event that took place about 2,000 years ago that might be the reason people saw a very bright star that night. That seems to me like a pretty interesting thing to do, but I don't think it would totally explain why the star is in the story and why the Christmas star has remained so fascinating to us down to this very day. I think one of the reasons the star fascinates us so much is that all of us like the idea of something that could guide us through the tough challenges of life. I'd certainly like to have something like that in my life—something that would guide me, give me direction, tell me where to turn.

Let's consider for a moment on this Christmas Eve that we all really do have a star to guide us. Not a physical star, necessarily, but a kind of inner wisdom that is always there if only we pay attention to it. If we think of the star as our inner wisdom, then I think it gives us a fresh new way to hear the Christmas story. Let's think about the three kings for a moment. Maybe what made them so wise was that they were willing to follow their star. They were willing to follow their inner sense of what they most deeply wanted to do; they followed their inner wisdom, their star. Perhaps that's why we think of them as wise.

So where does this inner wisdom take us in life if we're wise enough to follow it? Well, the Christmas story says it takes us to the scene of the birth of an amazing, wonderful child, a child who in some sense will be able to save us and to save the world. What does that mean? I think it means that when we follow our sense of inner wisdom, it leads us to a sense of rebirth, of new hope, of innocence and wonder—all of the things we think of when we think of new babies. It leads us to a sense of joy, of celebration, of feeling like we can make a difference in the world.

Even after the three wise men found the child, they still had one more decision to make. King Herod had asked them to let him know where the child was so he could come and worship him. But the wise men were warned in a dream not to do that and to go home another way. Once again, they listened to their inner wisdom and not to the voice of an external authority who they could sense was not trustworthy.

So let us become truly wise this Christmas—wise enough to follow our own star, to hear the voice of our own inner wisdom, to follow our bliss, so that we can find the new birth within our lives. The Christmas story says that even at the darkest times of our lives the star, the inner light, is still there, and if we follow it, we'll find new life, new peace, a sense of hope, and a sense of meaning in our lives. It doesn't say that the journey will be easy or that we will always get exactly what we want under the tree. But it does say that there is a journey to be made, a star to follow, and that at the end of the journey, there is something extraordinarily precious to discover—something like the birth of a child, full of possibilities, hope, and a sense of how miraculous it is to be alive. ∞

sermon writing

fireplace burns
coffee brews
thoughts arrive
energy stirs
senses wake
ideas form
ink flows
words emerge
pages fill
passion grows
spirit moves
(sometimes not)
sermon happens
peace comes

—Michael Brown

To order a copy of this book, send an email to:
office@peoriauuchurch.org

Visit the church website at www.peoriauuchurch.org